AN EXPLORER'S HANDBOOK

AN EXPLORER'S HANDBOOK

An Unconventional Guide
for Travelers to Remote Regions

CHRISTINA DODWELL

Facts On File Publications
New York, New York ● Oxford, England

AN EXPLORER'S HANDBOOK

Copyright © 1984, 1986 by Christina Dodwell

Library of Congress Cataloging in Publication Data

Dodwell, Christina, 1951–
  An explorer's handbook.

  Bibliography: p.
  1. Travel—Handbooks, manuals, etc.   2. Outdoor
life—Handbooks, manuals, etc.   I. Title.
G151.D62 1986   910.4   86-2142
ISBN 0-8160-1402-7

Printed in the United States of America

10 9 8 7 6 5 4 3 2 1

First published in the United States of America in 1986 by Facts On File, Inc.
460 Park Avenue South, New York, NY 10016.

First published in the United Kingdom by Hodder and Stoughton.

Contents

Introduction

This book is for people such as campers, walkers and travellers who want to know how to fend for themselves in the wilds. It is handy to be able to make use of the things about you. It is very satisfying to discover there is a lot more you can do for yourself than you thought and that living off the country is an art form with many options. So often, too, it is taking care of the little things that makes all the difference between a happy state of wellbeing which allows you to enjoy the experience of travel, and miserable debilitating discomfort which makes you wonder why you set out in the first place. There are also times when looking after yourself is not just fun, it is crucial. It can mean all the difference, not always perhaps between life and death, but certainly between going on or going home with your tail between your legs.

I learnt wisdom the hard way, though I must admit I enjoyed the process. The beginning for me was over seven years ago, when I went for an overland holiday but became stranded in West Africa. I found myself deep in the bush, with another woman and our newly-chosen means of transport, two rather wild horses. Lesley and I knew nothing about survival, we had no tent or camping equipment (except water-bottles), and no food supplies. We were relying on being able to buy food in markets and villages, but the land turned into semi-desert, villages were scarce, then none at all, and for about a week we had nothing to eat. It felt like an eternity. Within a few days we were riding listlessly, staring at the hot stony sand passing beneath us. When I looked up I saw only the scorched sterile dusty plains; nothing stirred because there was no breeze. My senses seemed to close up. We were both obsessed by our hunger, we talked for hours about our favourite dishes, and at night we dreamed about feasts and banquets. Had we known about the nature of the land I am sure we could have found something edible. Lack of water was an even greater danger, because we did not know how to look for it. And this is why I decided to learn to live off the land.

By the time we reached a village I doubt we could have gone much further. The villagers had little food for themselves but they gave us what they could—some maize, a handful of peanuts, and yoghourt, made from milk, fresh blood and urine.

Although that was the end of our ordeal, for me it was just the start of a three-year journey through the African continent, mostly alone on horseback. And in the seven years since that beginning I've been travelling extensively in Papua New Guinea, Central America and South-East Asia, studying whatever catches my interest. I've talked to bushmen and primitive villagers, game rangers and white hunters, commando troops and old timers, gypsies and farmers. I've lived in their villages, been out hunting with them and learnt of course not everything but at least something about how to survive in the wilds—enough to keep alive the pleasure of travelling hopefully to distant and inaccessible places. And what more can one ask?

1 *Methods of Transport*

Each different style of transport provides a separate way of experiencing the world, and each has its own advantages and disadvantages. Although a motor vehicle allows you to cover great distances with comparative ease and comfort, you are enclosed, seeing the journey through windows which even if they're open, do not bring the same spacious feeling as walking or riding. Travelling on foot alone or with an animal forces you to develop an awareness of the nature of the land, and inevitably it brings you into frequent contact with the local people. This can be rewarding, surprising, entertaining or instructive by turns.

Best Foot Foremost
For maximum enjoyment of foot travel one needs to discipline oneself to travelling as light as possible. Pack the heavy things at the top of a backpack to make the load easier to carry (on the same principle as loading a horse). Travelling in a group of three or four can be useful for sharing out the camping gear, but less useful for hitching lifts.

Being on foot allows one to climb or scramble up rock faces that vehicles and pack-animals cannot climb, and to cross river ravines using fallen trees as natural bridges.

But then of course there are limitations of distance covered. You either need all the time in the world or not a very ambitious ultimate destination. I'm not sure if there's a lot you can say usefully about walking mileage, except to discover your own comfortable daily limit on both level and rugged terrain before you leave home, then allow for a change of temperature, and if you're aiming for a destination by nightfall, allow some spare mileage for getting lost in.

Travelling with Pack-Animals
Pack-animals which walk slowly, unless they're running away, can provide a maddeningly dilatory experience.

Donkeys—may only cover 8 to 10 miles (13 to 16 km) per day. At best they walk about 2½ mph (4 km) for 10 to 12 hours a day. They can carry 150 lb (68 kg), but the heavier the load, the slower they walk. Speed and distance also depend on the terrain.

Mules—can generally travel at 3 mph (5 km) for 14 hours a day. They're much tougher and stronger than horses, and more disease resistant.

Horses—can walk at 4 mph (6½ km) for 8 hours a day, carrying 200 lb (91 kg). With luggage strapped down the horse can trot, triple and canter, though weight governs speed, and mileage is also affected by the overall length of the journey. In a three-day trip (not just walking) a horse can cover 150 miles, but when travelling over weeks or months my average dropped below 20 miles (32 km) per day. Time must be included for rest-days, and several rest-stops during daily travel. It is important to unload all luggage during rest-stops, otherwise the horse's back doesn't get dried out or rested.

Ponies—have all the advantages of horses and are more nimble and hardy. Their weight capacity depends on their size; 160 lbs (72½ kg) is all right for a pony of 14.2 h.h.

Yaks—travel at 1½ mph (2½ km). In Tibet, sheep are also used as pack-animals; they go in flocks and stay healthy in almost grassless country where yaks and ponies can't find food. Maximum load per sheep is about 25 lb (11½ kg).

Dogs—In polar regions, dog-sleds provide transport. A seven-dog team can pull a load of 600 lb (272 kg) and cover 20 miles (32 km) per day. There should be one person to each dog team, but it takes quite a bit of skill to learn how to handle them.

Camels—A sturdy camel carries 600 lb (272 kg) with ease. It walks at about 3 mph (5 km), covering 17 miles (27 km) per day. Its speed and distance are better if it marches by night and rests by day.

Elephants—are interminably slow walkers, especially if you are jungle-bashing. The only time my elephant went fast was as she skipped her way down rocky mountainsides.

To obtain pack-animals—go to where they are common; look in small town marketplaces, or ask in villages. Bargain over the price. Do not expect to be able to sell the animal later for the same price, somehow it never works out like that. But however bad the re-sale price, it is usually cheaper to buy than to hire an animal, though hiring would include a man to tend and look after the animal, a job which can be very hard work.

Riding and leading—The frustrations of leading pack-animals when you're on foot are compounded when you try riding one and leading another. Some of my experiences were trying to lead an obstinate donkey from the back of a half-trained stallion; later, trying to lead an East African zebroid pack-mule; and riding an ex-bucking bronco leading a camel. The day I set off leading the donkey from the stallion went like this: we made a late start and it was the rush hour. The dusty town streets were crowded with bicycles, carts, an assortment of motor vehicles, and many pedestrians. The donkey kept stopping. Every time it stopped I was dragged backwards along Diablo's back desperately trying to make him stop as well, but he only wore a halter and reins I'd made from string, and the string broke whenever it was pulled too tightly. Diablo bit the donkey. I lengthened the donkey's lead-rope, but at every tree the donkey swerved around the other side, which made me drop the rope. Dismounting to retrieve the rope was a bad idea since I had no saddle or stirrups and could not easily remount. Fortunately at this stage there were plenty of people to pass the rope back to me.

In the outskirts of town we got lost, then came to a muddy open drain which the animals refused to cross. In the chaos of refusals, circlings and shyings away, the rope got tangled and the donkey bucked until all the luggage fell off.

That donkey didn't travel with me for long; it ran away one night in a storm and I was happy to be rid of it.

In later travels I discovered that semi-wild or badly behaved animals can often be surprisingly well behaved if they're being led from a similar type of animal.

Luggage on pack-animals—In different parts of the world people have slightly different ways of putting luggage on animals, according to the type of animal, load, and terrain to be crossed. Use the local method wherever possible. One simple system is using two suitcases of the same size and weight. Rope their handles together so that they form an A-shape over a straw pad on the animal's back.

To improvise panniers find two sacks and cut the side-seams to halfway down, making smaller bags with large flaps. Stitch together one flap of each sack, overlapping them to form panniers. The weight should be kept as high as possible, and equally distributed between the two bags. To close the bags, pin the loose flaps together with a sharpened twig.

A third sack can be stuffed with dry grass or straw, and stitched to make a firm cushion to pad the animal's back and prevent sores.

A pack-saddle is strongly recommended; it protects the animal's backbone, and can be easily made from two boards of wood connected by arcs of iron, 1½ in (4 cm) wide and ¼ in (½ cm) thick, with hooks inserted on either side for pack-bags to hook on to.

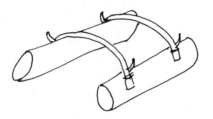

Girths and an all-round cinch help to stabilise the load. In mountain country it is generally necessary to add a crupper from pack-saddle to tail, to stop the load sliding on to the animal's neck when going downhill. Full tack is illustrated below. Straps can be made of cloth, leather or soft rope.

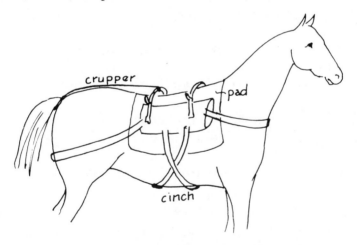

Hauling two full sacks on to a pack-animal can be tedious and difficult. Not being as physically strong as a man, I found a system which works well. By kneeling down and putting my shoulder under the centre join of the sacks, I could raise myself and the sacks up until standing straight, using my hands to help pull myself up with a stirrup, the mane, or anything handy. Having my hands free was useful also for patting the horse's back, telling him to expect the luggage. Standing by the horse's shoulder with the bags on my outside shoulder, I push the rear bag over the horse's back and settle it in place, then step out so that the other bag hangs in place.

The weight in the sacks should be evenly divided, or the load will slip; and heaviest articles should be packed at the top, so that the strain is taken by the strongest part of the horse's back, over the withers (shoulders) and just behind them. Behind the saddle lie the animal's kidneys, usually a weak area.

Travel on Horseback
Horseback travel is among my favourite methods of exploration since it gives a clear view over the surroundings; the land meets the sky all around, while ahead the horse's mane and his alertly pricked ears are a continuous bond with reality. A horse is strong enough to carry me and luggage (in saddlebags) across territory that I could not cross on foot, and to cover larger distances, varying his speed between walking, trotting and cantering. When the journey includes swimming across rivers, a horse is a strong swimmer, enabling me to get across some wide rivers in flood.

The disadvantages of horseback travel are responsibilities such as the frequent need to find fodder, the chance of the horse going lame, or straying away overnight, and the necessity of having rest days.

Obtaining a horse—Look for the hardy type which knows how to look after himself, and is still fat after the winter. A point to consider is that white-coloured hooves tend to go lame more easily than the tougher black hooves. A mountain-bred horse often knows how to manage difficult terrain and sniff out marshes, while a stabled or meadow-kept horse tends to trip over things, not watching where he puts his feet. A thoroughbred is often not very clever at foraging for food.

I seldom have much choice when looking for a horse, as it depends what I find in the wild, or on a ranch, or in a slaughter-yard, among rejects and unrideable horses.

Sometimes a horse is given to me because it seems worthless. But it loses its bad habits early in the journey, and the fact that you are the only constant in the everchanging landscape, I find, tends to create a closeness and feeling of trust between you.

The horse I bought in a South African slaughter yard was a neat hardy bay with no vices. I knew nothing about how to bid at slaughter-yard auctions so I asked the dealers, rag-and-bone men and butchers there for advice, and they helped me to avoid buying some potentially disastrous animals.

A police pound may occasionally have a stray horse available for sale, or ask about bands of wild horses at big ranches and outback places.

A standard way to catch a wild horse is by getting helpers and driving all the horses into a makeshift corral. The horses you don't want should be allowed to escape. Then try to get a rope or two on the horse you want to keep, or use a dart-gun. Bear in mind that an old wild horse is very hard to train, and a semi-wild one is much easier than a totally wild one.

Saddlebags for solo horse and rider—difficult to buy, but easy to make. Each time I make new ones I try to improve on the design. The best material I found was lightweight waterproof canvas, or the nylon flysheet from a tent. Sew the material using extra-strong thread and making many seams in stress areas to form two large satchels with pockets on the front and back end pieces to hold things which are continually needed, such as water-canteen, camera, map and compass. The satchels can be joined together by strong straps that fit over the saddle.

If you need to improvise a buckle, use twine and a small stick:

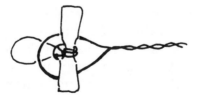

An all-round cinch helps to stop the saddlebags flapping about when cantering. Things that bump around are likely to frighten the horse.

The swag of Waltzing Matilda's jolly swagman is another saddlebag variation. It is a long package formed by rolling all one's possessions into a blanket, which is carried over the front of the saddle.

Tack—When I was not able to buy a saddle, I made one from a strip of carpet with two tightly-rolled pads of underfelt to raise the carpet over the backbone of the horse, leaving it free of pressure.

Instead of a bridle, my horses usually travel in a halter with rope reins. A bit does not seem necessary for a solo horse.

A useful extra is a flyband, which I attach like a browband when flies are bothersome. The fringe of the flyband should hang well below the horse's eyes. The movement of the fringe when the horse shakes his head keeps the flies away from his eyes. A flyband can be improvised from fringed leather, or string; occasionally I use leafy twigs, the best being a variety of pine whose long-hanging needles make a fine fringe.

A Loftier View: Travel by Camel or Elephant

Obtaining a camel—Look in desert headquarters for retired army camels. Or ask nomads, but often they do not want to sell because their camels represent wealth; to their minds there is no point in exchanging wealth for money, especially since money doesn't last as long as a camel!

A camel's condition is recognised by the firmness of his hump, and by the fullness, not scragginess, of his neck.

One consideration when travelling by camel is the design of its feet. If they are designed to walk on desert sands and plains, the feet are very large and clumsy. Such camels are useless in rocky mountains; they cut their feet, stumble and sometimes fall over. However, mountain-bred camels have small feet; they are agile and steady. My desert camel made the journey over the mountains without too many problems, but he baulked at mud and rivers; he hated getting his feet wet.

Crossing the muddy sandy delta of the Omo River, we had extra trouble because in addition to streams and pools which seemed to lie in every direction, there were innumerable mirages and I couldn't tell the real thing from the mirage. We kept detouring to avoid streams that looked real until we came close up to them and discovered that they were not there.

To load a camel—When I bought a pack-camel I learned how to rope its load on, using four wooden poles, a straw cushion, and two grass ropes. It was an ingenious method because the rope acted as springy suspension for the baggage and held its weight comfortably on top of the camel's humpy back.

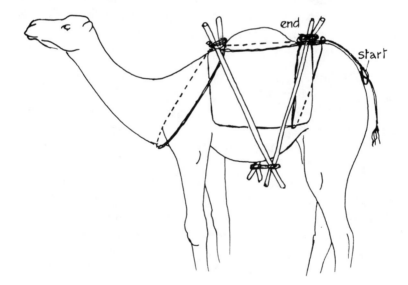

Rope One: start around tail as crupper, taut to front poles, round front poles, four times. Continue with a loose loop round neck, once round front poles tightly, then back to crupper rope and loop round it before going down and around the sack pad. Bring the rope up to the back poles, put it through and around many times then knot it.

Rope Two: this is the rope to secure the luggage and should be looped over the front poles and threaded under the back ones before slinging the weight of the luggage from the forks. Avoid loose clanking rattles; they'll upset the camel's nerves.

To drive a camel—Different tribes have different ways and words for controlling camels. For my camel I had to use Turkana commands. To make the camel lie down the command was 'Tu, tu, tu', and if he was feeling obstinate I had to rap the ground with a stick and hiss crossly at him. To make him stand up it was 'Ha, ha-ha, ha'. The command Ha was effective for most other general orders.

To make him hurry up and walk briskly it was usual to sing a camel-song, calling 'Ha, ha, brrr; hei, hi-ho-ha', in random tones, notes and sequences. When two or several people are doing this, it all blends together into a curiously beautiful melody.

To control an elephant—Again commands and ways will vary. Mine was not well-trained; she didn't know many commands and wasn't very obedient. To make the elephant lie down the command was 'Mello', shouted firmly. A tap on the head made her stand up. To ride, I sat on her neck with my legs tucked behind her ears, and directed her by tugging at either of her ears and flapping her earlobes with my toes.

The main problem is that it takes months of being with an elephant before it learns to trust a new handler, although experienced elephant-boys (*mahouts*) seem able to change between beasts as required.

Paddling Your Own Canoe

Travelling by canoe is a unique experience, and has advantages over animal travel in that a canoe does not need to eat, nor to rest, and it does not usually stray at night.

When buying a dugout canoe bear in mind its age, because old canoes tend to leak. No big problem, just plug the leaks with clay or putty. Larger leaks and splits can be patched by flattening out a tin can, and hammering nails through it into the canoe. Use clay as the filler.

A fibreglass canoe or kayak is a good method of transport down rapid rivers or in coastal seas. A recent innovation is the use of virtually indestructible polyethylene, instead of fibreglass which is more easily broken. Mending holes with fibreglass and resin is a sticky messy business. Carrying the repair materials without seepage is a problem too, and some airlines ban them as dangerous cargo.

For Operation Raleigh, Colonel John Blashford-Snell is using open cockpit fibreglass canoes, designed like the Canadian canoes and very stable for novices. One problem with any type of rigid canoe is getting it to and from your put-in and take-out places, though of course it is easily carried on a car's roof rack and ideal for day trips.

Foldaway canoes (rubberised canvas stretched over a wood and metal frame) are designed for travel simplicity, packing away into two bags which weigh a total of about 66 lb (30 kg).

Inflatable canoes of PVC reinforced with polyester can be durable enough to meet army specifications. They pack up to the size of a suitcase and weigh about 55 lb (25 kg).

Rafts
Apart from rafts of empty oildrums or inflated inner tubes, which may not be floating handily by, the traditional desert island escapee would use natural resources. You build a wooden raft from logs held together by pairs of cross-poles, which sandwich the logs between them. Use pegs to keep the cross-poles in place. Cut notches where the bindings will go.

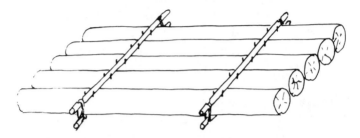

Bindings can be creepers, briers, woodbines or vines.

There are various designs of raft. A useful method of attaching single beams is with a strong supple stick bent over the beam and pegged into holes in the framework.

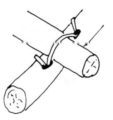

Some trees float less well than others, and the buoyancy of any raft depends on the specific gravity of its timbers. Oak and ironwood logs tend to sink.

Bamboo rafts float well. Use many poles of bamboo tied into long bundles joined by cross-poles, or else a few bamboo poles which are lashed into the shape of a field gate with two diagonals. This makes a very serviceable raft.

Reed rafts, made from bundles of reeds, are an emergency alternative.

Internal Combustion

A motor vehicle has numerous advantages in terms of shelter, weight allowances, escaping from dangerous situations, and long-range travel. Factors for consideration, such as type of vehicle, type of tires, maintenance tools and spare parts would make a book in themselves. (See Appendix 2.) For advice about overland vehicles and all motor expeditions I recommend the Automobile Association of America (see Appendix 2). They provide an extremely helpful and efficient service.

Hitch-hiking—is certainly a good way to meet local people and one tends to learn the language quickly, but it has risks and disadvantages. Weigh them up. What I really like about hitch-hiking is the way the world changes with each new ride, be it a battered Land Rover, an air-conditioned limousine or a truckful of old tires with room for me on top.

The Guided Tour

Guides are useful if you need to reach a specific destination without wasting time getting lost on the way. Having a guide means that you are no longer responsible for choosing your direction, speed, or evening destination. It is more like being a passenger. Your main responsibility will be to look after him, his health and sometimes his food.

In some places a guide is also a porter, but in others a guide would charge extra for carrying baggage or expect you to hire someone else as well. In countries such as China there are set rates for the job. In other places haggling is an art form. Fix the terms for rations and pay before you set out. For rates find out what the missionaries or government patrols pay.

One guide-porter seldom goes a long distance, but can hand you on to others when he reaches the edge of his tribal territory. This is because

(a) the man doesn't usually know his way outside his territory
(b) probably he can't speak the languages of other tribes
(c) he is likely to be afraid of returning alone, regarding all other tribes with suspicion and mistrust.

My first pair of guides in New Guinea were neolithic-type men who wore wild pigs' tusks through their noses, and carried bows and arrows in addition to my backpack which must have weighed about 55 lb (25 kg). As the porter puffed uphill, his breath whistled out down the pig's tusk.

2   What to Pack

In an emergency bush materials can be used to make substitutes for plenty of things. When caught without shelter in a rainstorm, try using a banana leaf as an umbrella. Pawpaw leaves make a substitute tobacco, and boiling the roots of flowering yucca can give you soap, while general purpose rope can be improvised from many natural sources, from vines and roots to seaweed and horsehair. See Chapter 16 for more ingenious alternatives and details of how to go about achieving them.

If the journey is going to be short, I can do without most things, but when it will stretch for months I want to take a bit more with me. Some items can be bought along the way. I tend to avoid towns and look for farms or village markets. However, many items that are difficult to find or expensive in other countries are best obtained before setting out.

Without some sort of checklist what to pack can be a terrible problem, and if you collect everything you think you will want, you'll probably be staggered by the amount. Literally staggered if you're backpacking. So just sit down quietly beside the pile and go through it item by item, asking yourself: Do I really need this? If the heap is still too big, repeat the performance, asking: Can I live without this? Only the barest minimum is totally necessary, the rest is either semi-useful or clutter. Not for many today is the leisurely encumbered travel of the Thirties when Robert Byron set out on his road to Oxiana with the conviction that while travelling one should consume three new books a week and a bottle of wine a day. Though I do believe in taking one book. You can keep swapping it along the way and find yourself reading some surprising and enlightening works as a result.

The following is my checklist, divided into seven sections: Everyday Essentials; Bush Cookery; First Aid Kit; The Clothes You Stand Up In; Making Friends; Documents; Essential Extras.

Everyday Essentials

Sleeping bag—necessary even in the tropics; mountains and deserts can be cold. Down bags are warmer, but when they get wet the down goes into wadges. The bag is not ruined if you take the time to fluff it up again. To be warmest in a sleeping bag you should take off your clothes. By keeping them on, your body-heat cannot circulate properly in the bag. I prefer a full zip type since on freezing days it can be opened and worn as a blanket.

Sheet liner—useful on warm nights, and protects you from crawling insects, though not from the biting kinds. To make a liner, sew a cotton sheet into a long tube. Stitch the bottom end to make a sack.

Something to sleep on—Most people associate a hammock with luxurious indolence, but for me it often simply made the difference between a good night's rest or miserable discomfort. It kept me clear of rough ground and rocks, ants, creepy-crawlies, or wet ground on rainy nights. My hammock is nylon, weighing only a few ounces and it packs up no larger than a clenched fist. Sleeping in the air is cooler than sleeping on the ground, and in mosquito country I hang the mosquito-net so it tucks into the sides of my hammock (with my sleeping bag below me to prevent mosquitoes biting from underneath).

Occasionally I've travelled with a foam mat of high-density foam only ½ in (9 mm) thick. It provides good insulation from cold or damp ground, and gives a surprising degree of comfort. You can also buy self-inflating foam mats. Foam mats weigh little but are bulky.

Tent—Many people carry a small tent. Perhaps this is a good idea, as it can be dry and insect-proof, but for myself I wouldn't like it in the tropics or wherever. It would spoil my pleasure at sleeping under the sky, watching the galaxies move, seeing the night around me, and being part of it all.

Sheet of plastic or Space Blanket—for a groundsheet or to improvise a shelter from the rain. A Space Blanket is a sheet of metallised plastic. It is supposed to work like insulation and keep you warm on freezing nights. Unfortunately whenever I've used mine it has developed condensation, not insulation, on the inside which dripped down making me cold and wet. The most lightweight ones fold up the size of a cigarette packet.

Mosquito net—when a mosquito net is necessary, it is invaluable. The lightweight nylon ones don't always keep mosquitoes out but they are cooler to sleep in than the fine weave cotton nets which are popular in swampy areas. Cotton nets, made in China and obtainable from Chinese trade stores or equivalents, are very effective against mosquitoes, but they are bulkier and heavier to carry than nylon nets.

Light—With long twilight, a light may not be necessary. But on the Equator there is no twilight; when the sun goes down at 6 pm the night takes over. Your light can be a candle, or a jar of kerosene with a wick in it. Some campers carry Tilley lamps, or have attachments to their cookers. Take a torch as well, but don't forget that in tropical climates batteries go dud quickly.

Flick-lighters and spares—They also make good gifts.

String and nylon rope—at least 33 ft (10 m) of two different grades. Nylon ropes have a specific breaking point, so I buy a grade of rope strong enough to hold the weight of whatever I'll be tying. My hammock ropes are little thicker than string but they don't break unless they get frayed. Even the horse's tethering ropes are less than 1/2 in (1 cm) thick. A tether rope that I made into a bitless bridle for my South African horse was borrowed one day by a tractor for towing a car and laden trailer up a hill. The rope didn't break. But it never looked like a bridle again.

Climbing ropes and ones which get frayed over sharp surfaces need to be thicker, especially if your life depends on the rope. To stop the rope-ends fraying, burn them with a match.

Hunting knife—I prefer a lock-blade knife, not the kind of penknife that could close on my fingers. Knives should be kept sharp. Sharpening stones can be borrowed from workshops or village metal smiths. A long strong bush knife or machete is useful for jungle bashing and lighter than an axe.

Catapult—fun, and sometimes scores for the pot.

Fishing line and fish-hooks—you don't need a rod, which is difficult to carry anyway.

Self-adhesive plastic tape or insulating tape—useful for mending things.

Needles, thread and safety pins—including some extra-strong waxed thread.

Plastic bags—things packed in plastic bags don't get wet; and the contents stay together.

Water bottle—holding 1¾ pints (1 litre).

Water purifying tablets—not pleasant tasting, but handy when camped in populated regions. (But see page 69.)

Map and compass—Michelin maps are excellent. Make sure your compass is accurate before you leave home.

Bush Cookery: Equipment
This is the backpacker's minimum:

Billycan—is light and more practical than a cookpot with a long fixed handle or small side handles. A billycan has a wire loop handle by which it can be suspended over a fire from a green pole held up between forked sticks. A wire loop handle is also convenient for oven baking and easy for packing away. A small billycan is not much use except for boiling water for tea or coffee. For cooking the most versatile size is a diameter of about 6 in (16 cm) and 2½ pint (1½ litre) capacity. Nests of billycans which pack inside one another are useful for group travel. Spare billycans are never wasted. They can double for pot roasting, mixing bowls, baking tins, soaking basins, etc. Some sets are non-stick. Make sure the lid is tight fitting for steam cooking and when burying the pot in hot ashes or a ground oven. It is usually deep enough to double as a frying pan. For preference, get a non-stick one.

A fuel-saving idea is to paint the bottom of your cook-pot black, since it will absorb the heat more readily and speed up the cooking process. If it has a gloss finish, sandpaper it to take off the shine.

Heavy duty tin foil—has a multitude of uses. See Chapter 8.

Soup-dish type plate and mug—enamel not aluminium, as the latter gets too hot to hold.

Fork and spoon

Can opener—though I just use my knife. Take a corkscrew and bottle opener if you want them.

Cooking stoves—Most campers carry a cooking stove and spare fuel. But see Chapter 8 for how to build your own ground oven.

Indeed most extra cooking gear can usually be improvised when it's needed. Big leaves will act as extra plates. A small forked twig, peeled and sharpened, is a fork. For a spatula or stirring spoon, use a wide stick shaved flat at the bottom, or a flat strip of bamboo. A whisk may be made from a bunch of stiff twigs, tied tightly. A sieve could be a piece of mosquito netting. A bottle makes a reasonable rolling pin (doesn't need to be empty). A closed fir cone works as a lemon-squeezer.

Motor campers for whom weight is less object may like to add one of the following:

Pressure cooker—apart from the familiar domestic advantages, it is particularly good for tenderising tough meat and for speeding up the cooking of dehydrated foods.

Waterless cooker—looks like a pressure cooker but it works more like an oven. It can be used with or without water in it. It is a non-burnable cookpot with a wire mesh at one level for baking bread or roasting meat, and above that are other containers for steaming.

Dutch oven—the original ovens brought to South Africa by the Dutch settlers were cast iron. Now they are aluminium but still heavy. A useful sized one weighs about 12 lb (6 kg). They stand on three stubby legs just clear of the hot embers, or on an asbestos mat on top of a gas or primus stove. The lid has an upturned brim which can support hot embers or charcoal for greater heat.

Other useful extras—if you have the room for them are:

Long serrated knife and short sharp kitchen knife
wooden spoon
metal collander
chopping board
non-stick frying pan
large plastic mixing bowl
thermos
coolbag (insulating bag)
airtight plastic containers—square ones for neat storage
Clingfilm and a roll of plastic bags
rubbish bin liners
kettle—some camping shops sell ones designed to boil
    extra fast
teapot
bucket
pot scourers and J-cloths
clothes pegs
fly swat

plastic 5 gallon cans—for water storage. Put a bit of sheet plastic under the cap to prevent leakage. Or keep water in expandable water bags (from camping shops). If the water develops green algae, wash out the container with sand and water.

And if it exists, buy a book of the country's local recipes.

When stowing supplies in a vehicle, it is worth the effort of doing it carefully. Rough roads can cause chaos. Despite our careful storage for crossing the Sahara, our Land Rover was jolted so violently that the pop-top containers popped their tops and flung their contents out; screw tops became unscrewed; glass jars were broken, tins of food split or exploded, and the food cupboard was soon lined with a sticky mess of cooking oil, tea leaves, soap powder, spices, sugar, rice and broken glass.

Here are some hints that we should have benefited from. Decant all things out of glass jars. Sticky things such as jam, honey, ketchup or margarine travel well in plastic squeeze-tubes. These re-usable tubes, filled from the bottom and sealed with clips, are available in camping shops. Keep all the tubes in one box.

Keep all packets of food together in a bag or box. Use rubber bands to hold things shut. Remember that cardboard boxes don't last well and plastic bags wear out. Always use two bags at a time.

You don't need to take full packets of things. For small quantities use empty film cannisters or plastic medicine vials. Remember to label everything.

Bush Cookery: Food Supplies

The next list is intended to show you some food options which are lightweight, non-bulky, nutritious and tasty. Some items can be bought in any supermarket or chemists, but some are only going to be found at specialist sources or expedition suppliers. Don't take everything on the list, just note what you fancy. I think that the only essential is salt.

Instant coffee

Tea bags

Powdered milk—pellets are sometimes available.

Sweeteners—artificial ones are far lighter and less bulky than sugar. But brown sugar could be a worthwhile luxury.

Salt—maybe also buy some butter flavoured salt, which adds butter-flavour to vegetables and is available from American-style supermarkets.

Pepper—a tiny amount is sufficient.

Mixed herbs and spices—tiny quantities of things such as curry powder, ginger, nutmeg, cinnamon. They hardly take up space or weight, and they make all the difference to bland food. And I sometimes put them in my tea.

Citric acid—crystals of concentrated lemon, from the chemists. Or use a Jif lemon.

Orange powder—gives a good start to the day.

Muesli, or oatmeal

Nuts, raisins and dried fruit

Rice—and/or instant potato, or spaghetti.

Powdered soup—good for making sauces, stews, etc.

Stock cubes—for flavouring stews and gravy.

Pulses—dried lentils, soya beans, kidney beans, chick peas.

Dried meat and dried vegetables

Cooking oil

Margarine

Dried egg powder

Flour—take a bit for thickening stews, for dusting before frying, and for making bread-like goodies.

Baking powder—very small tin.

Mustard powder

Tomato crystals, or concentrated tomato puree in a tube

Dried bacon bits—from supermarkets. Add to soups, salads, sandwiches, vegetable or egg dishes.

Cheese—buy processed cheese in tubes. Or dried cheese like Parmesan.

Chocolate powder—cooks well. Health-food shops sometimes sell concentrated chocolate substitutes (like Carob).

Vinegar powder—Make it yourself by soaking one cup of rice in five cups of vinegar overnight, then cook the rice in vinegar, and dry it slowly in an oven. When dry, crush the rice to powder. To re-obtain the vinegar, soak the powder in water (ratio 1:5) for an hour.

Tinned food—tinned meat and fish are useful but heavy.

I prefer to take minimal supplies, and buy local produce along the way. Buy little and often rather than stocking up. Use what's in season, and shop at the markets.

For the provisions you want to get in advance Appendix 4 lists the names and addresses of recommended expedition suppliers. Some expedition food is only sold in catering-size packs which are more than a small expedition needs. Smaller quantities can be bought from Cash and Carry warehouses.

First Aid Kit
My first aid kit consists of:

Anti-malaria pills
Insect repellent
Antihistamine cream—small tube, for insect stings
Antiseptic cream—small tube
Antibiotic cream—small tube. Tetracycline is a broad-spectrum cure.
Plasters—assorted sizes
Pain killers—very powerful ones
Tiger Balm—a product of the Far East that can be bought in many Indian-owned shops throughout the world. Use it for relief of sprains, muscular aches and pains, headaches, insect bites, and general itches. Thoroughly recommended.

When we set out from England with the Land Rover we had a fully comprehensive first aid kit. We used none of it for ourselves, though it was handy for treating people who came to us asking for help. Fortunately, most of their problems only needed cleaning, antiseptic and bandaging; it can be dangerous to dispense stronger medicines ignorantly. Beware of young men demanding to be given pills—they weren't ill, and they didn't care what the pills were for, they just believed pills made them stronger and sexier!

The Clothes You Stand Up In

Also the clothes you wear to scramble through scrub, wade rivers, ride horseback and sweet talk the authorities.

Footwear—Open sandals keep feet cool in hot climates. But jungle boots made of canvas are a blessing in thorny or muddy country. The advantage of canvas over leather boots is in being lightweight, and when wet, they dry quickly in front of a fire.

Clothes—Most travellers in cold climates know to take obvious and adequate precautions with their clothing. But even in the tropics you may need a warm pullover. Jeans or shorts for men answer most needs, but in many parts of the world women face special problems of propriety. The sight of women in shorts can disgust people who believe that female thighs should not be exposed in public. Shabby scruffy clothes will affect people's attitude toward you; if you look respectable, you will be treated with respect. In Third World countries I usually travel wearing a long skirt, which is cool, comfortable and convenient. It protects my legs in brush and thickets. For mountain-trekking I just tuck the back hem over the front waistband to make instant pantaloons.

A *sarong* is an exceedingly useful article of informal clothing for both men and women. It is a long wide cloth which you wrap around your body, from waist to knees, or chest to knees. Sarongs are worn in many different countries. In rivers or places where you can't bathe naked, wear a sarong.

Best bib and tucker—remember that in the most unlikely places you may, as the visiting foreigner, find yourself bidden to some extra special festivity, from royal banquet to village wedding, for which the civilities require you to appear to have made a sartorial effort (for me one example was meeting the Queen of Thailand). An extra pretty crease-resistant long skirt in some material that folds up small is the answer for women, and for men a tidy pair of trousers is useful because jeans are sometimes inappropriate and may be banned.

Sun protection—a sun hat, plus maybe sunglasses and sun-tan cream. Lipsalve for dry climates and maybe cream for your skin.

Toilet bag—soap, towel, hair brush or comb, pocket mirror, nailfile and clippers, toothpaste, toothbrush and dental floss, a small bag of washing powder and some shampoo, and multipurpose toilet paper.

Making Friends
The old colonial image of the wicked trader bamboozling the simple natives with a handful of beads dies hard. *The Beagle* in which Darwin sailed to Tierra del Fuego took bonnets to soothe the savage breasts of the Alacaluf Indians. But there is no getting away from the fact that suitable presents make you friends and repay small or large courtesies along the way. Here is my tried and tested checklist of what to take:

Dictionary of national language (if available)—In my experience phrase-books are more frustrating than useful. If I don't want to say exactly what they've said, I'm stuck.

Photographs of home and family—Remote people love to see pictures of where you come from, and this is a good form of communication. Photos of snow get interesting reactions in the Tropics. Take a few spare pictures to give away.

Camera and plenty of spare film—If you have an old Polaroid camera take it as well, since people are usually thrilled to be given their picture; and they'll be more relaxed in the photos you take afterwards with a standard camera. Some older Polaroid cameras use b/w film which is much cheaper.

Trade goods and gifts—tend to be more useful than money in remote places. The most successful trade goods and gifts I've used are tobacco, flick-lighters, pens and T-shirts. People can say what they like about tobacco, but it is undoubtedly a widely-enjoyed commodity, and sharing it with a group promotes goodwill. Tobacco may be bought by the handful very cheaply in many market-places; some tribes smoke leaf tobacco, others prefer chewing tobacco. Less remote villagers smoke cigarettes. Share some between the old folk when you sit listening to their stories.

Safety pins, pocket mirrors and big-eyed needles are also highly prized. Salt is another useful gift, but it is heavy to carry.

Decorative beads are often treasured by men and women, and never mind the colonial overtones.

Sweets are a good way of saying thank you when you've taken photographs of people, especially children. But be warned, on the overland routes campers have indiscriminately handed out presents and given sweets to the children. All across the Sahara route the children came in crowds to our Land Rover, and stood beside it shouting at us to give them presents. The shouting became louder and louder, their faces distorting with rage because I wouldn't give things to them. Don't think that by giving to them you can make them leave you alone. They'll go away but only to tell their friends where to find you.

Documents

Passport—Keep your passport with you at all times. Take a photocopy of it and keep it somewhere separate. While you're photocopying, make copies of your driving licence and birth certificate too. You never know . . .

Take about 20 extra passport photos to use for visas en

route. Some countries require several photos per visa application. Get visas in advance if possible. Watch their expiry date. Take along your student ID card and your Youth Hostel card if you have them.

Money in travellers' cheques—take some small denominations such as $10 or $20 for times when there's no bank. Keep a sum of cheques in reserve for any emergency where heavy bills might be incurred. Being independent means being able to look after yourself. Immigration officials often demand to see that you have enough money to support yourself during your stay. Extra travellers' cheques are necessary if, like me, you tend to cross borders by land and do not have an air ticket out of the country.

Air tickets—are usually required as evidence that you are a *bona fide* bird of passage. An alternative is an airline MCO (miscellaneous charges order) which can be used as a ticket from anywhere. It needs renewing yearly and can only be refunded by the issuing office.

Health insurance—can be a good idea. The Health Insurance Association of America can provide information. Their address is: 1850 K St. NW, Washington, DC 20006.

Health Certificate inoculations—check what you need a month before setting out. For information contact the United States Public Health Service at the International Health Care Service (see Appendix 3).

Try not to let essential certificates and visas get out of date. Mine for Indonesia had expired and the Chief of Immigration told me to catch the next plane out of the country. There was only one flight a week from Jayapura but it went to Papua New Guinea so I bought a ticket. It wasn't until I was about to board the plane that someone demanded to see my Health Certificate. He thumbed through to the cholera vaccination stamp, which was out of date and he refused to let me board the plane. The immigration also refused to let me stay in Indonesia, and the pilot refused to let me fly. Tempers rose and soon everyone was shouting angrily. Everyone that is, except me, I sat quietly in a corner and prayed that I'd be allowed into Papua New Guinea, after travelling for eight months just to get there. The pilot won the argument and the plane went without me. As it left, a customs officer looked in my passport and noticed that my entry permit to Papua New Guinea was due to expire the very next day.

I had twenty-four hours to get into Papua New Guinea, or my visa would be invalid. And my last hope had just roared into the sky.

It felt as though the bottom had just dropped out of my world, after eight months of travel it seemed that the door was to be slammed in my face. After several hours of visiting doctors and immigration, the chief of immigration arranged for me to leave Indonesia at 6 am the next morning, using the coastguard's canoe. It took me to Vanimo, a small outpost at the back end of Papua New Guinea. A happy ending, but I don't really recommend leaving things that much to chance.

Car documents—Special documents (Carnet/Green card) are necessary for vehicles travelling abroad. For advice, contact the Automobile Association of America (see Appendix 2). Don't forget your International Driving Licence.

Documents for animals travelling over international borders—Veterinary certificates of an animal's fitness and general good health are needed in addition to certain inoculations against animal diseases. Each international border requires exit and entry papers for each animal. Actually I didn't realise this until after I'd taken a horse across several borders, particularly since when riding cross-country, the borders are invisible, perhaps a mountain ridge or a river, which I'd crossed unwittingly. Only once did I have to stand before a national Chief of Police who thumbed through my passport and shouted

'But there is no visa!' By pure chance, my horse and I were staying the weekend at the President's home, and the President told the Chief of Police to give me visas for as long as I wanted. You don't always get that lucky.

Inoculations for a horse against horse flu are advisable in Eastern and Southern Africa, and against tsetse-carried sleeping sickness. The inoculations are more effective if divided into two parts, separate jabs with a week between them. A word of warning: after a horse-flu inoculation the horse should stay quiet for at least two weeks; if he runs around and gets into a sweat, the extra strain on his heart may cause heart failure.

Essential Extras

Spare parts for motor vehicles—Different types of vehicles have different weaknesses. Advice about spare parts can be obtained from motoring organisations or the AAA (see Appendix 2). I would also refer to them for advice about kit for snowy places.

Finally don't forget pens, notepads and the odd pencil (pencil will work on damp paper); envelopes and un-stamped aerogrammes. A handbook of edible local plants with clear illustrations will give you confidence when using Chapter 15 to supply the cookpot along the way.

3   Looking After Travelling Animals

To Shoe or Not to Shoe

In rocky country, ranch horses and those which have never been shod do not need shoeing because their feet are tough, whereas horses which are unshod in grass fields have softer hooves. When a horse is left out at grass for years its feet can splay out and it may be impossible to trim them enough for soundness. Splayed feet tend to crack easily and go lame.

The advantage of a hardy horse without shoes is that his hooves seldom need any maintenance. They get worn down by the terrain, being ground by sand and pebbles, thus keeping a neat shape.

Hooves which are shod require maintenance every 4–6 weeks, since the hooves grow, like toenails, becoming long and clumsy, and likely to throw a shoe. Even if the shoes have not worn thin they should be removed and the hooves need to be filed back into the correct shape. My preference is for short hooves, the nails placed as high as practical, and with some nail-spaces left to give greater spring to the shoe.

Hot shoeing ensures a better fit than cold shoeing, but both are a skilled process. Farriers can be hard to find, so carry extra nails for emergencies.

Daily Care

Hooves—Horses' hooves (if shod) need to be picked out with a hoofpick or stick every morning. In snowy country it is necessary to pick out the hooves more often to prevent the snow being packed into ice-balls and causing lameness.

Grooming—Brush the saddle area. In cold weather a horse doesn't need grooming since the natural oils and dust will help to keep him warm.

Bathing an elephant—Looking after elephants included letting them take a bath every day. Hours of walking through the mountainous jungle makes them hot and grumpy, and as one would expect, they like to bathe and cool down. My elephant's favourite baths were in rivers or lakes deep enough for her to lie in; if we couldn't find a river she made do with a stream, using her trunk to suck and blow the water over her back. Her baby elephant enjoyed streams enormously. His favourite game was to squirt all the water out of rockpools on to the banks.

Dust baths were also part of the elephant's daily routine. Mine used to hurl the dust around herself to stop the flies biting (some flies can even penetrate an elephant's skin!). It is important to brush the dust off the saddle area before saddling the elephant, to prevent soreness.

Wounds and Saddle Sores

If you let sores break through the animal's skin they are unlikely to heal during the journey. To help avoid saddle sores make sure its back is clean and dry before saddling; use a saddle blanket; take frequent rest stops, unsaddling often. Wash all wounds clean with salt water (or sea water); use antiseptic such as Gentian Violet; keep the wound clean, dry and free of flies by using a cloth bandage.

Ticks

Dip-baths—are a good way to get rid of ticks, which can cause general loss of condition, fever, or death. The simplest ways to dip-bath a horse are either by using a bucket and sponge to rub the liquid well into the animal's coat, or using a farmer's spray race. The spray race is designed for cattle and is a long narrow passageway with spray coming from both sides. It can be frightening for the horse if he has not been in one before, but it is harmless. Don't let the horse run through too fast or his coat won't absorb enough dip to be effective. Let him dry off in the sun. Don't walk through a spray race yourself as the liquid is powerful and I found that even my hands were allergic to it.

The old established farm type of cattle-dip is a deep sunken trough which the cattle jump into and swim through. I wouldn't put my horses through a trough-bath because they could hurt themselves by jumping in awkwardly (safer to take a bucketful for a sponge-bath).

The dip should be effective for about a week, depending on rainfall and proliferation of ticks. Some farms where I stayed had to dip their cattle twice weekly.

Tick-grease—I like to keep a small jar of tick-grease, using it in the horse's ears, round the base of his tail and around his fetlocks (ankles) to stop the ticks climbing up from the ground.

Picking ticks off by hand—if you see a tick biting, pull it off. Hold the tick's body lightly but firmly between forefinger and thumb, and pull it sharply. Check that the tick's head is attached to its body; there is danger of infection or fever if the head breaks off.

Tethers and Hobbles

Tethers—Animals may not understand about ropes or tethers unless they are accustomed to them. A tether can easily make a loop which the horse steps in, and when he pulls the rope tight around one of his legs he may panic.

A small group of horses usually won't stray if one or two mares are tethered (or hobbled).

A tethered horse needs plenty of rope since much of the grazing area gets trampled by his hooves. The safest way of tethering a horse yet allowing him a good circle of grazing is by tying him on a long rope to a springy branch high up on a tree. The higher the branch, the longer rope can be used (giving more grazing area). The rope should not touch the ground, being a few inches short of it, so that the horse won't easily step over the rope and get tangled. By using a springy branch the horse can pull the branch downwards and reach for fresh grazing.

Another method, on flat ground or where there are no trees, is to tie the rope to a stake or skewer at ground level, but this sometimes causes tangles.

With two horses sometimes I just tie their neckropes together so that they can graze nearby, unable to run away since the rope would catch around rocks or trees.

Neck-ropes—My horses usually wear neck-ropes—a long rope with one end tied loosely around the horse's neck. When the horse is grazing the neck-rope trails on the ground and if he treads on it, it reminds him not to stray. Ranch horses are often trained not to stray. A neck-rope also means that the horse is easy to catch, with 20 ft (7 m) of trailing rope. Nylon rope is strong and lightweight. When travelling, the rope can be coiled up as a lasso, or used as reins.

Hobbles—Hobbles tie two of the horse's fetlocks (ankles): either both front fetlocks (best) or front and back on the same side. If you tie the diagonal front and back the hobbles will not be effective since a horse walks with diagonal hooves simultaneously.

Some people hobble horses by tying their halter rope to one front fetlock, short enough so the animal's head is lowered (he has to pick his head up to run) which is fine if he is only grazing but no good if he wants to sleep or doze.

Hobbles shouldn't be painful, so make sure they don't rub.

An Afrikaaner gave me a length of rawhide, told me to oil it until soft and supple, and showed me how to tie it to improvise hobbles. Double the rawhide and slip the ends round one leg and back through the loop formed by the doubling. Leaving 6–8 in (15–20 cm) free, encircle the other leg with the ends, making a turn, and fasten the ends with two half hitches.

Hobbles can also be made from a stirrup leather, by putting its middle around one fetlock, then twisting it half a dozen times and lastly buckling it around the other fetlock.

People often assured me that horses cannot run in hobbles, but when one of mine got freaked out by the camel, he went galloping away, bounding along with his front feet tied together.

Hobbling camels—When you are confident that your camel won't stray far, make it lie down and tie a string around one of its bended front knees, tying the knee bent double. The camel can stand up and hop around on three legs to browse foliage. However, it can stray quite far on three legs and it's sometimes necessary to tie both of its front legs bent. But then you must remember it can't browse, so provide it with fodder.

Grazing and Fodder

Grazing—Animals which are raised in tough dry surroundings usually know how to scavenge for grass, dig for roots, or dig for water. Animals raised in soft conditions do not have the same abilities or hardiness.

If the animal is only walking or the journey is short, I generally let him live off the land, provided the land has reasonable pasture. Overlush grazing will give a horse an upset stomach. I let the animal enjoy the lush grazing for 2 or 3 days then pull him back to drier pasture.

In some fields used by cows the grass looks lush and green, but it is sour tasting, having been manured by cowdung. After the first few mouthfuls my horse would drift around hungrily but refusing to eat.

Look at the types of grasses that your horse likes to eat. His favourites are probably the most nutritious ones, like wild oats. Animals like to vary their diet with different kinds of grass—they will even go off horse-cubes if fed them too repetitiously. Some countries have poisonous types of grass; learn to identify and avoid them; horses unused to the terrain may eat it by accident.

Fodder—When I am asking for speed and high mileage from a horse, it needs some additional, more concentrated fodder. If this can be found along the way, so much the better. Xoza, my South African horse, had diet supplements of maize, sugarcane stalks and leaves, lucerne, sweet potatoes, cattle fattener and dry porridge. At one farm where we stayed, Xoza was to be found among the dairy cows at morning milking, waiting for his turn to eat cow-feed in a stall, then at noon he joined the chickens eating corn, and at teatime he'd be outside the farm door waiting for cake or biscuits.

It is useful to know how to make a hot bran mash, which is best fed the evening before a day of rest. Use 3 lb (1.35 kg) of bran in a bucket, 1 tablespoon of salt, 2 tablespoons of molasses, and pour on enough hot water to make the mash wet. Cover the bucket with a sack and leave it to cool for 20 minutes.

Oatmeal gruel is good for a tired horse. Put a double handful of oatmeal in a bucket, add water and mix to a paste.

Any type of soaked and pounded grain can make a mash or porridge. When feeding oats, bruised oats are more digestible than whole oats. Musty bran causes coughs and wind troubles.

To cure coughs try using hay tea, made by putting hay in a bucket and pouring boiling water on top. Cover the bucket with a sack and leave it to brew.

Camels—Camels browse and graze from treetops to groundlevel. Although they can last for days without water, they must eat daily. Dry straw is better than nothing. Having several stomachs, a camel needs time to chew the cud. During a long march when you have to choose between a day's stop for browsing or an extra day without water, choose to stay and browse. The size of the camel's hump tells you how he's bearing the journey. When the camel's fatty reserves are used up, his hump will go almost flat.

Elephants—An elephant has a voracious appetite, consuming about 441 lb (200 kg) of foliage daily. One problem I had with mine was when she spotted someone's banana tree she not only took all the fruit but she ate the whole tree as well.

Horse to the Water

You can take a horse to water . . . but if there is no way for him to get down to the water, he cannot drink. There was no room on my horse for a bucket. A foldaway canvas one would have been useful. With Xoza I improvised a bucket from a thick plastic bag, but I had to hold it while he drank. My next horse was afraid of the plastic bag and, despite knowing that it held water, he would not willingly drink from it until he became used to the idea.

How often to water an animal—This depends on what he's used to. Some horses are used to going without water during the day, and this is all right if you will be able to find water in the evening. If he's used to frequent water, let him drink when he wants. But the more he drinks in the heat of the day the more he'll sweat it out. It can be harmful to let him drink when he is very hot, or after a big meal of grain. Make sure he drinks before he eats a feed; if he eats his fill then drinks, the grain in his already full stomach begins to swell.

Camels have to be trained to last for long periods without water. Training is achieved by gradually building up the length of time between drinks, which eventually can stretch to months. Without water training, a camel should drink every fourth day. When working very hard in hot weather, a drink every third day is enough. In cold climates where green food is available, the camel is content to work for two weeks without water.

Cross-Country Hazards

To cross rivers—Underwater sandbars can make the difference between easy wading and a deep swim. The sandbars are formed by the action of river currents. The bars don't go straight across bends, they follow the direction of an imaginary line connecting the inner bank on one side to the inner bank of the other.

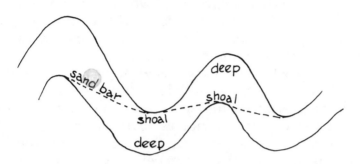

River estuaries are easier to swim across at the mouth, rather than trekking upriver or trying to swim through marshy lagoons. At estuaries of fast-flowing rivers, it is often worth waiting for low tide when the water becomes calmer. The high tide also has a calmer half-hour, but may have disadvantages such as sharks coming in with the tide to feed at the river mouth.

To swim across a wide river local people often use a buoyancy aid such as an inflated animal hide. Goatskins are used in the Tigris, and ox-skins which can support about 220 lb (100 kg) are popular elsewhere. Alexander the Great and his troops were said to have used distended hides stuffed with hay.

In Africa, hollow hard-shelled gourds are popular as floats. Some people use two gourds tied on to a pole; pack your gear in the gourds and sit on the pole to paddle across. When crossing a raging river in New Guinea I used a local float of three short logs tied together with vines, which I held with my hands while swimming with my legs and feet. The advantages of such a buoyancy aid are that it will keep you afloat, it is less tiring and will keep your luggage fairly dry.

My system for swimming across rivers with my horse and luggage is to put the luggage and saddle on a large sheet of plastic, tie it into a well-wrapped bundle and attach it to a long rope. Putting the bundle at the water's edge and holding on to the rope's end, I lead the horse into the river, walking at his shoulder on the downstream side, so that when swimming I won't be swept into his legs. It is considered a bad idea to ride on the back of a swimming horse, and as a general rule one swims at his side or by hanging on to his tail. To steer him from his tail end, splash water forwards with your right hand to make him veer left, or splash left to go right.

A horse usually swims far more strongly than a person, and in my experience horses love swimming. While swimming in fast water, keep the horse's head pointing slightly upriver to prevent him being swept too far downriver. The bundle will float across behind you; I don't see why it doesn't sink, but none of mine ever have yet.

Fences—It is wise, if you can find him, to ask a farmer's permission before you ride across his land. You could be accused of trespassing. Loose wire fences can sometimes be pulled down to the ground, or pinned low so the horse can step or jump over them. Horses cannot see wire so if you want the horse to step over wires, put a wooden pole along the top wire. Don't cover wires with grass since the horse may try to brush through it.

When a horse won't go through or over a hazard, it may be easier to dismount and drive him from behind. Keep hold of the end of his long neckrope, or leave him free to manage alone, yelping to encourage him forward.

Mud—Regularly, the horse and I used to flounder in deep mud at riverbanks or in marshy areas. Keep him walking forward, don't let him stop. Sometimes my horse stood still and I couldn't make him move as he sank in deeper. He had to be urged into fighting his way out; gentle coaxing seldom had any effect, while excited cries and fierce yelps often did the trick.

If the mud is serious enough to warrant turning around (not easy) and going back to solid land, then you should never have attempted it in the first place, and your horse will become mud-shy. I've never turned round to go

back, but I have had to run for help when my horse sank
to his back in mud. He gave up struggling forward, and
everything I did failed to make him fight his way out.
It was midday, I was ill with tick-bite fever and had to
run for miles to reach a farmhouse. The farmer didn't
understand my urgency, and it was an agonising half
hour before I returned with sacks and ropes and helpers
to free my horse. After an hour we freed him, and
fortunately he was unhurt and none the worse for his
experience.

One would assume that an elephant would have diffi-
culties in deep mud because of its weight, but this is not
so. Nature and evolution have designed the elephant to
cope. As the elephant steps downwards, its weight makes
its foot slightly shorter and fatter, and when it pulls its
feet up the foot becomes more elongated and thinner,
sliding easily out of the hole. Thus an elephant seldom
gets bogged down in mud.

4   Tested Exits from Tight Corners

This is going to develop into a chapter of accidents, so let's start by thinking constructively about how to avoid some of them.

Communication
When you have got a language barrier to cope with it is more important than ever to be polite and smile and say good morning in any language rather than none, though it is not difficult to pick up the local salutation.

When people greet you, return the greeting, or greet them first. Travelling slowly on country paths and roads, I tend to greet those who see me passing, but if they don't see me I won't disturb them. After a greeting, if the people ask me a question which I can't understand, I simply tell them the name of the place I am going, and where I am coming from—places close by that they should recognise. Showing your map can be interesting to those who have been to school, but don't expect them to understand it or be able to give you directions to places on it.

Without a common language you can communicate by showing objects like photos or maps, or by making sketches. (Ask people's permission before you sketch or photograph them, as sometimes they don't like it.) It is usually clear from people's tone of voice if they are threatening you, warning you or greeting you. By being a polite foreigner, you will be more readily forgiven for unwittingly causing offence.

How Not to Offend Local Customs
Customs vary, and things that are considered rude in one culture may be meaningless gestures in another. In

Buddhist countries it is rude to sit with your feet pointing at anyone; it is vulgar for a woman to put her hands on her hips; while in social gatherings, men tend to get upset if a woman sits on a taller object and her head is higher than the men's. Also remember that while avoiding the eye of the person you're talking to in the West gives a shifty expression, looking someone full in the face while conversing in the Orient is considered bold and rude.

Travelling in remote parts is no time to cling to women's lib principles, though it surprised me how far some people went to make you conform to their customs. On my arrival at an isolated pearl-trading village in the Indian Ocean, the women led me to a hut, took away my clothes and dressed me as one of them in a sarong and blouse. They smeared my face with white powder, and around my neck and wrists they clasped strings of pearls that came from their local oyster-beds.

European girls and women wearing short shorts are being offensive by baring their thighs in public in most countries from Turkey eastwards, and generally among primitive peoples too. Don't show off your body unless you intend to be sexually provocative.

In villages where men live separately from women there may be men's paths which women are not allowed to use. This taboo does not generally apply to white women, who are considered as some kind of un-categorisable freak, but it is best to ask first.

Local Hospitality
When you stay overnight in a village it is a good idea to go and greet the headman or chief, otherwise he may feel snubbed. Shake hands with everyone and smile a lot. Shaking hands is a useful gesture of goodwill. It can take away tension and makes people well disposed toward you.

In a Zulu village I stayed with a splendid old man; we couldn't understand each other's language but he told his grandchildren to catch a chicken for our supper. After cooking it we sat down to eat, and an angry man barged in through the doorway. He was wild with rage because I had not asked for his permission to be there. Power games aren't just a Western invention. So I jumped up smiling, shook his hand warmly and praised him for having a friendly village, saying how proud he should be of the old man, whose behaviour was a credit to the village, and so on. Though I knew he probably couldn't understand my words, he certainly could hear my tone. After that, there was no problem.

Where possible repay people's kindness with gifts.

One couple I met were having problems because whenever they made a pot of tea or coffee they felt obliged to offer some to everyone in the house, which no one ever refused, and their supplies were rapidly running out. What they hadn't realised was that it is often rude to refuse something that is offered, so people automatically say yes. Depending on my supplies, my system was usually to offer cups of tea at least to the man and woman of the house, and to whoever had offered food to me. Any tea left over was put in a big mug to be passed around, and I'd explain that I didn't have much. Don't show all your supplies; people don't often understand the concept of keeping for tomorrow what you could enjoy finishing today.

Camping in Hostile Country
In hostile country territory, it is better to stay overnight in a village, or camp well off the road where you will not be found. The same people who would rob you in the bush are honour-bound to protect you and your possessions if you stay in their village. (And there is a saying, 'It's safer inside the lion's jaws'.) But don't unpack, it creates unfair temptation for people who have little. If you leave your knife on a rock, it is really your fault if it disappears.

Carrying Weapons
A long sharp machete can double as a weapon. Crossing lion country once I did take a flare gun because lions

like horse meat, though I never needed to use it. But I don't carry firearms for various practical reasons. If you are crossing a number of international borders you can get a lot of official hassle over a gun. Also, should a sudden emergency arise, ask yourself whether the gun would always be close to hand or packed away somewhere? And remember, if bandits attack and see that you have a gun, it will be something they will want to capture at any price. Life is cheap and guns are valuable.

Man Eats Man

The likelihood of being harmed by cannibals is very small. I have encountered them several times and never felt threatened. In parts of the Congo Forest cannibals can be recognised by their teeth which are filed to points. Some that I saw were like sharks' teeth, others were filed into double points.

The reasons for cannibalism are varied. The Fang tribe in Gabon and the Kukukuku in Papua New Guinea do it for protein, it is easy meat; others do it to gain the strength of the slain; while tribes such as the Tugeri have cannibal rituals for the baptism of a child. The Fores did it out of love, eating the decomposing flesh of their dead relatives in order to free the spirit from the body. They believed that unless this ritual was followed the spirit would be trapped and doomed to eternal limbo. Unfortunately for the Fores, the decomposing flesh was often contaminated by Kuru (Laughing Death), a fatal disease carried only by humans. Its occasional recurrence shows that the old ways die hard.

Small Town Troubles

Crime naturally gravitates to towns and it is up to you to take sensible avoiding action, such as not walking alone down dark alleys on the local payday, and keeping cash and passport in a body belt or an inner pocket to deter the chance bag snatcher. Pole fishing with a bamboo pole and hooks through the window of your room at night is a local activity in some parts of Africa. It's not wise to grab the pole, since it may be implanted with razor blades.

I travel with the belief that the deeper I get into remote bush areas, the safer in general it becomes. Country people's code of conduct is stricter.

In the Sepik region of New Guinea, I didn't have any trouble until I reached the small town of Pagwi, where someone stole my canoe. It was only a paddle-canoe but it was my transport, it meant a lot to me and I was determined to get it back.

With help from Pagwi's government officer and some locals I did recover it, but a few days later it was stolen again and this time I was held prisoner as a spy for a week. After I'd got my canoe back I paddled up a tributary to a lake in the mountains. There my canoe was stolen for the third time. Some fishermen told me it had been taken by a man from across the lake, and a village elder said he would help me. He went up onto the hilltop and yelled out across the water, 'Hey you, whoever took Christina's canoe, bring it back right now.' And it came back that day with no problem.

In another small town, Ambunti, I asked the government officer about the usual sort of crimes in his district, and he said the most common ones were assault, spreading false rumours and use of malicious magic or sorcery. The local prison consisted of a few huts with a small wire fence around them. I asked if many people escaped, and got the answer that no one bothered to run away. But I noticed some rows of big new fence posts. 'So why are they building a second fence?'

'Oh, that's because the prisoners get too many visitors. The new fence is to keep people out.'

In Bandit Country
Bandits often turn out to be just a group of men seeking an opportunity for robbery. Sometimes in primitive parts of the world a woman is in less danger of attack than a strange man who represents a threat to their territory.

On the other hand, women have occasionally to cope with the amorous bandit. My method of dealing with both the mercenary and the ardent is similar and is based on the superbluff. There is an awful lot you can do to disconcert the opposition and you should always keep talking. Don't antagonise them, or behave violently since it may provoke greater violence.

Alone on foot, encountering ruffians I'll sometimes use a combination of politeness and deliberate mis-understanding—maybe shaking hands with them all and saying how pleased I am to see them, could they just help me make a fire. And during this I find out their names or the name of their home village. Once I know the name, I should be safe, and I tell the men that they must not rob me because I will inform their chief or village headman. Sometimes I tell them that my husband is a large and jealous policeman, and he's waiting for me in the next town. Name-dropping of local chiefs or the president can be helpful. I've even thrown in Queen Elizabeth for good measure.

Surprise is the essence of self-defence. In South Africa, after I'd swum with my horse across a river, we were lazing in the sun to dry off, and my saddlebags were on the ground semi-wrapped in a large sheet of plastic. A tribesman saw us and swam over. He reached our shore and ran towards me, naked and yelping with excitement. He reached out to grab me. But I had snatched up the sheet of plastic and thrust it stretched out as a barrier between us, and said, 'Here, fold this up.' He wavered, not able to grab me through the plastic so I said again, 'Fold it up', and handed one end of it to him. To my amazement he did begin folding it. So I made a quick pile of other things for him to fold while I saddled the horse. I even got him to help me put the saddlebags on, just by giving him orders in the same tone of command.

But then he did grab me, got me in a bearhug, and was saying something over and over, saliva drooling down his chin.

Fortunately the horse caused a distraction by taking

a few steps away. So I said urgently, 'My horse, I must catch my horse', and kept insisting vehemently until he let go of me. It doesn't matter how silly your excuse or demand, so long as your voice has conviction. As I recaptured the horse I sprang into the saddle and we galloped away.

In primitive regions you can sometimes frighten away would-be attackers by pretending to be an ancestor spirit or a ghost. Simple folk are easily spooked. Hiss and chuckle, pretend to be a lunatic. It frightens people. Paddling down the Congo River with my companion Lesley, we'd deter the advances of ardent young men by paddling in unison, staring straight ahead and chanting funeral dirges.

Despite my several encounters with robbers and ruffians, they have never harmed me physically, nor have they ever stolen all my belongings. And twice I got angry enough to make them give back what they had stolen!

Getting Arrested

Not a good idea in the Third World, especially if there's no American embassy. Indignation can be effective, as long as it's low-key. Don't use words like ridiculous; it can make people unreasonably angry. In Oriental countries it is very important to avoid making anyone, even junior clerks, lose face. Again, a bit of judicious name-dropping sometimes helps. Make sure you know the name of the president. If all else fails, I just act inane until they give up harassing me.

Getting Arrested as a Spy

In Third World countries a spy can be anyone who is in the wrong place at the wrong time. Many men have no clear idea of what a spy *is*, but they glory in the importance of catching a suspected one.

Find out who it is that you must convince of your harmlessness. Act generally happy and formally polite. Don't resent everyone because of a few big-heads; while

under arrest you need friends. Have an urgent reason—
such as a sick father—why you need to continue quickly
on your way.

In the Congo when Lesley and I reached Brazzaville by
canoe the authorities tried to arrest us as spies. They
couldn't understand that we were just tourists and I
couldn't understand the officer's French well enough
to know what was going on. So I suddenly demanded,
'Come, see we are tourists, see canoe' knowing that our
canoe was of a design unfamiliar to any they would have
seen. And I marched toward the doors. Some soldiers ran
up to grab me but when I repeated 'Come, see canoe' they
simply followed. We all marched down to the dock, to
where Lesley and I had tied our canoe to a big boat. But
the boat wasn't there, and there was no sign of our canoe!
Fortunately it was found at the public canoe parking-lot
later in the day, and Lesley and I went on our way.

Town jail would be a very bad place. Being arrested in
the bush is not so bad. Twice I've been held captive, both
times for a week, then was set free unharmed.

Being Harassed for Bribes

Some countries are particularly corrupt (mentioning no
names; you'll find out if you're in one). Police or army
at the roadsides can flag down cars or pedestrians for
examination of papers. In the bush, I usually demand to
see their official papers first and write down their ID
number; it spoils their game. In town, some people pay
bribes by keeping bank notes folded discreetly inside
their passport or driver's licence. It is more like the idea
of a tip in the west. Find out the correct rate to bribe
in advance. There is a surge in demand for bribes at
Christmastime.

Personally I seldom pay bribes unless in big trouble,
because I think it makes people greedy and corrupts
their moral values. On my travels there is usually no
hurry. The delay at police roadblocks for checking
documents can be whiled away pressing wild flowers,
writing letters or mending things. I always behave

politely and answer questions helpfully (though not in-variably truthfully), but don't let anyone hold on to my passport for longer than necessary. Make sure that your documents are not out of date, as this can be an offence.

Vehicle Breakdown
For pre-expedition advice about breakdowns, what spares to take and how to cope in all motorised emer-gencies, see Appendix 2.

Wild Animals
Wild animals seldom cause problems for travellers. Certain animals, including wild pig, buffalo and bears, are known to be more aggressive, but most animals simply run away. Few animals attack unless they are frightened, cornered, protecting their young, or rabid.

On foot don't run away from animals; they'll chase you just for the fun of it. Walk away without showing fear. If you accidentally corner a wild animal, always give it the chance to escape. Lions are not maneaters unless they get a taste for it. They prefer zebra, buck or horse. A leopard stood up in front of me one day, block-ing my path and angrily swishing his tail. I retreated cautiously, watching his tail, not his eyes (lest he see my alarm), and I acted angry too, stomping my feet heavily as I retreated, pretending that I was big and powerful. As soon as I was out of his sight, I fled. But I didn't stop to check my direction and so missed the place where I'd tethered my horse. It took me ages to find him again.

On foot I've escaped from wild pigs by climbing trees. Hikers in bear country often carry bear bells which jingle as they walk, warning any bears that may be using the same path. I've only ever got seriously mauled once, by a jackal; the attack seemed unprovoked but doubtless the jackal had a reason.

Getting Lost
When asking people the way, beware. If you ask 'Is this the path to X?' the answer may be yes because they think

it is rude to disagree with you. Remember that the local names for places are sometimes different from both the English name and the name written on the map. A Zulu village called Hole in the Wall was locally written as Hluhluka and pronounced Shlshleker.

When lost in the jungle without a compass, mark your trail by breaking off green twigs and leaving them in your path.

In more open territory it is still hard to walk in a straight line unless you line up a landmark and, before reaching it, you look for another landmark directly in line beyond.

A broken compass can be useful. Keep the magnetic needle; it should still point north if you put it on a leaf or a wood-chip in a bowl of water.

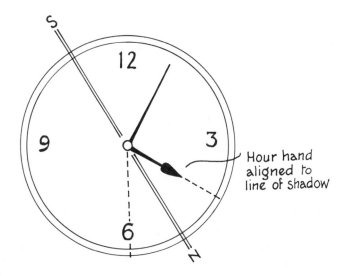

Hour hand aligned to line of shadow

With a watch you can work out approximate compass directions by combining the time with shadows cast by the sun. Put the watch flat, and turn it until its hour hand is pointing in line with the shadows. At noon in the northern hemisphere the shadow lines point north. At any other time of day, north will be halfway between the direction of the falling shadows and the 6 on the watch face. If you've only got a digital watch, you can still get an idea of the direction by looking at the length of shadows which are shortest at noon.

Other ways of telling direction are by looking at the moss on rocks and trees. Moss and lichen grow on the side which is exposed to moisture-bearing winds.

To navigate by the stars at night in the northern hemisphere, locate the North Star (Pole Star of Polaris) which lies 1° from true north. It doesn't change position during the night since it is in line with the earth's axis.

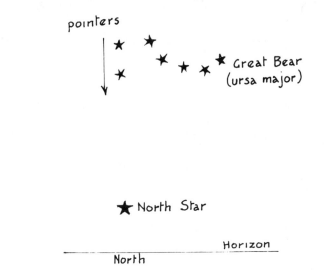

If the North Star is not visible, look for the Great Bear or Plough and calculate where in the sky it would have been when its pointers were vertical; when vertical they point north.

In the southern hemisphere, use the Southern Cross. In the equatorial and tropical belt, use Orion and Antares which lie east and west.

Lesley and I had no map or compass when we undertook the horse journey in West Africa. Our direction lay wherever seemed most beautiful or interesting. It occurred to me that we awoke lost, were lost as we travelled, and stayed lost at night. But it would not have made any difference if we had known where we were. Over the years I have worked on the theory that if you have no specific destination in mind you can't be lost. You are only lost if you fail to find somewhere specific, or don't get there on time.

5   Making Camp

Camp Sites
Select a place to camp bearing in mind your requirements. Do you most need water, firewood, shelter from wind and rain, or freedom from insects, or a place of sheer beauty?

The priorities will vary according to your method of transport. To have fresh water nearby is very useful; but if there are stagnant pools you could get besieged by mosquitoes. It is wise to camp upstream from farms or villages; downstream the water is polluted. Valleys tend to be cold places at night, and misty in the mornings, while higher ground may be bathed in early sun.

To avoid mosquitoes and insects, camp on high ground open to any breeze. Don't camp in marshy areas and places of long damp grass. Willow trees denote insects and misty chill. (For relief from insect bites, see Chapter 17.)

A cosy sheltered dell could become a puddle if the night turns rainy. Especially at wet times of year, find a dry site with natural drainage, and check from which way the rain should come. (Moss and lichen on trees and rocks usually grow on the side facing into the damp weather.) Look for the umbrella of leafy trees. But of course beware of tall solitary trees if thunderstorms are likely. Ash trees are reputed to attract lightning. It is true that if an elm, oak or poplar is struck by lightning the sap blows up, and tends to explode the tree.

Equally unwise in a thunderstorm is to camp under a rocky overhang or in a cave mouth. The ionisation of the air by the rocks, as in metal, can pull lightning to it.

In tropical and mountainous country there is the added

danger of flash floods. It is very tempting to camp in dry riverbeds; I have often done so myself, lured by a trickle of water and green grass for the horse.

Waking up lazily one morning I dozed and idly watched the rain clouds venting their wrath on the mountains up beyond my camp. I felt glad I wasn't in the rain. Then suddenly I realised this would be the path of the flash flood. I have never de-camped so fast in my life. Flash floods give no warning; all you hear is a distant rumble, and the next moment the flood is upon you. Reaching the safety of high ground I stopped to see what would happen. The air was ringing with the chirring of cicadas, my horse became restless and his ears flicked towards a sound I couldn't hear. Then I heard the roar as a foaming wall of water came racing down the riverbed. It was easy to believe that flash floods can sweep away trees, bridges and cars.

Having chosen a camp site, decide where to make the fire and where to sleep. The fire should not be within sparking distance of dry grass and undergrowth. Do not make the fire upwind of a good sitting-area—smoke gets in your eyes may be a good tune but it's no fun.

Shelters

In bad weather natural windbreaks are provided by fallen trees, rocks, and anything with a sheltered lee-side.

The most easily constructed shelter is simply a plastic sheet stretched from a fallen tree to the ground, and held in place by heavy rocks. Equally simple is to drape the plastic sheet over a raised string or pole and weight it to the ground on both sides like a ridge-tent. Nearly always you can find a tree or a rock to serve as a strong upright for one end, and for the other end, if there's no suitable second tree you can use two poles crossed and tied at the top. The poles won't fall over if you loop the string over them and anchor its end to the ground further away. Failing any solid uprights, make a trestle, or ridge-tent shape from poles tied together.

Rope can be improvised from vines or a strip of supple

bark. String for tying poles together can be of bracken-stalks, grasses, creeper, or a shaving from a long green stick.

Without a plastic sheet (or spare blanket)—any kind of ridge-tent shape or lean-to can be made and thatched with leafy branches to keep out the rain. To thatch the sides you will need to put several branches slanting up to the cross-pole; stick their bottoms in the ground and tie their tops to the cross-pole. Weave the thatching branches between these bars. Any foliage will do for thatch, though the bigger the leaves, the better. If the roof leaks and you intend to stay for several days, it could be worth plastering the outside with clay, not mud. In my experience mud disintegrates under heavy rain.

Also useful for a few days (and no more complex than putting up a tent) is a shelter made by tying together the tops of three or four springy saplings. Tie them firmly overhead and twist their branches together. Add extra branches. The top should be the most waterproof, but the sides can have less foliage to let a cooling breeze blow through. When you leave the place, break the string and the saplings will spring back to their own shape.

Sleeping Arrangements
Sand is lovely to sleep in. Wriggle until it fits your shape. Or sleep on a bed of heather which is bouncy and sweet-smelling. Other comfortable natural mattresses can be made from bracken, broom, evergreen branches, dry grass, dry moss, or any dry springy foliage. The man-made alternatives to assure a good night's rest include an easily rolled-up mat of high-density foam or, my preference, a nylon string hammock, and a sleeping bag (essential for all campers, even in the tropics) or a Space Blanket. The pros and cons of this equipment are detailed in Chapter 2.

I prefer a zip-up sleeping bag since it can be opened and used as warm clothing. (Several African tribes wear blankets during the day.) My sleeping bag is truly multi-purpose. It even came in useful when my horse floundered in such deep mud he could find no footing. I hauled the saddlebags to dry land and spread my sleeping bag out over the mud. The horse struggled forwards and my sleeping bag vanished in the bog beneath him, but at least it gave his legs enough support for thrusting him on to safe ground. While he dried off I went back into the bog (still tightly holding his rope so this time he could pull me out) and wallowed around until I found my bedding. Such a versatile piece of equipment deserved rescuing.

Tramps know the excellent insulating property of old newspaper. Scrunch it up loosely inside your sleeping bag.

If you have no sleeping bag, use newspaper scrunched inside loose-fitting clothes, and spread a few sheets of it over yourself. Or use dry grass, bracken or dry leaves in the same way. If you wake up freezing cold, let yourself shiver, it will warm you. Or try *gentle* exercise; avoid violent exercise since it is exhausting, and sweating will make you colder. Several times I've lost my sleeping-bag, and on one occasion I simply forgot it, going on up to 9,840 ft (3,000 m) in the mountains. The night air was perishing, but I was snug and warm, buried in a mound of dry grass with some hot rocks I'd heated in the fire.

With or without a bag the warmest place to sleep on a cold night is on the hot ground where your fire has been. A good idea is to push the fire on to fresh ground, about 3 ft (1 m) away (so you can feed it without getting up during the night, and it is easily revived for coffee in the morning.) Let the ground cool for half an hour before you lie on it, and if it's still too hot, cover it with a thick layer of earth or sand. The ground should stay warm all night.

Breaking Camp
On leaving every camp site, you should make sure that your being there has not spoilt the place. Broken glass and sharp tins are dangerous to animals; litter looks ugly

and it is unnecessary to leave it lying around. Burn or bury all your rubbish. Be certain that the fire is properly dead. Unless you're thorough, the fire won't really be dead for many hours and a gusty wind could start it up again. To kill a fire pull it apart, beat or stamp it out and throw water on it, then cover it totally with earth or sand.

6   Drinking Water

Water is not just something that comes out of a tap; it is
more vital than anything else to our existence. Nearly
three-quarters of our bodyweight is made up of water.
The average adult needs an intake of about 5 pints
(3 litres) per day in cool idleness; in the tropics a man
needs up to 10 pints (6 litres) a day. When working
strenuously your body needs an extra 1 pint (½ litre) for
each hour's work. Some of the required water is contained
in the food we eat, the rest we must drink. Lack of water
causes thirst, dehydration, constipation, tiredness,
dizziness, and so on. Dehydration is common when
you're travelling, so make a conscious effort to drink
more when water is readily available.

Human nature being what it is, most people only start
taking the idea of their daily water intake seriously when
they look like running out of the stuff. Thirst in deserts is
partly physical and partly based on fear. The combination
is agony. In these circumstances water training is vital.
Train yourself not to drink while you're on the move, not
even the odd sip. Only drink at dawn and in the evening
when you've made camp. It takes several weeks to get
used to this.

Every member of an expedition should have his own
water bottle. This should have a cover of felt or cloth
which can be wetted to cool the contents. Cured skins of
cow, sheep or goat can be obtained in parts of Africa,
which (like canvas waterbags) are hung outside the
vehicle during driving and the water keeps cool through
slow evaporation. Canvas loses about 20 per cent of
water through evaporation.

Many desert nomads suck small pebbles to keep their

saliva flowing. A tribe in Northern Kenya has the custom of inherited 'sucking stones', treasured objects which are handed down from mother to daughter.

The more you drink, the more you sweat. The Turkana people cover their bodies with ochre and animal fats to prevent water-loss by sweat. Turkana have little use for water: they drink camel milk; have no clothes for washing; and an application of body ochre is their equivalent of a bath.

To Find Water

In dry rocky streambeds listen for the sound of water trickling between stones. In dry scrubland look for greener or thicker vegetation, or a line of trees which may mark a water course. In the desert look for groups of palm trees. Birds indicate the presence of water. In thickets, game trails often lead to water but are very confusing to follow—beware of getting lost! In low-lying land, water may seep along beneath dry sandy riverbeds; sometimes the water is not far below the dry bed. Dig down to look for dampness. If you find the damp course, dig a bit deeper and wait for water to well into the hole. I've had to rely on this method in semi-desert, where sometimes the holes were as much as 3 ft (1 m) deep. Such water has been filtered pure by the sand, it is refreshingly cold and tastes great.

To dig for water without a spade, use a sharp-pointed stick; jab it repeatedly into the ground, then use your hands to clear away the earth.

In the desert some wells have a stone placed over their mouth to prevent them silting up; make sure you replace the stone after taking water. Wells seldom come complete with rope and bucket, and when you can see the water but have no means of reaching it, this can be excruciatingly frustrating. Local buckets are sometimes just a leather hide laced to a ring. In the Sahara some wells are over a hundred feet deep; looking down one is like seeing a small circle of sky at the bottom of a very long tunnel.

To Tell Good Water From Bad

Water from springs or deep wells is generally pure. Where streams are fast-flowing, or where rivers are slow but *deep* (taking water from midstream rather than the banks) water is usually safe, except just downstream from habitation. Always take water upstream from villages and farms, and remember that the chemical crop-spraying of farmland can poison the water. Water pools in a livestock area are not recommended, although they are less foul after heavy rain.

Rain water is naturally pure. Stagnant water is of course impure, but swamp water is often not stagnant; it may filter itself in an imperceptible slow state of motion, and so long as water from habitation does not drain into it, it can be safe.

The colour of the water may have nothing to do with its purity, but can simply be affected by vegetable dyes or minerals in the ground; drinkable water may be white, yellow, black, red, brown, sometimes cloudy, sometimes clear. Beside swamp forests in Africa I reached a region of gushing streams, coloured red-amber in the sunlight, and like Coca-Cola in the shade, cascading falls of it, fresh and bubbling. It was lovely to drink.

Muddy water is not necessarily undrinkable. If you fill a bowl with muddy water and let it stand for 30 minutes much of the mud will settle to the bottom.

Filtering water does not make it safe to drink, but simply removes the particles. To filter, strain the water through a cloth, or make a filter from a hollow branch (or bamboo segment) blocked with moss, sand, grasses, etc.

To scoop up shallow water without disturbing the sediments, improvise a cup by curling a leaf into a cone-shape, or use a hollow reed as a straw.

Ice and snow are generally pure, but eating snow makes you thirsty. To melt snow, pack it as densely as possible; loose snow requires more heat to melt it. Ice melts more easily than snow. Even so, melting the ice for cooking water uses about twice as much fuel as the food cooking. It helps to tilt the pot during melting. Drinking too much cold water may give stomach cramps. Don't drink water flowing directly off a glacier; the milky colour is due to very fine but sharp grit particles, which irritate and may damage your stomach lining. Filters, except expensive professional ones, aren't very effective against such fine particles; the best protection is to let it settle, which can take three days.

In North America beware of water holes without surrounding vegetation, or with scattered animal bones: the water could be alkalinely poisonous.

In Africa remember that most fresh-water lakes and rivers at altitudes below 6,560 ft (2,000 m) are usually infested by bilharzia. Bilharzia is caused by microscopic flat-worms carried by river snails which live in slow-running streams and water less than 1½ ft (½ m) deep. It can be caught by drinking, swimming, or wading through the water. When I started travelling I didn't understand bilharzia, so I caught it. I am told that the worm usually lodges in the liver where it can cause irreparable damage. But it produces no specific symptoms except tiredness and low spirits, is virtually undetectable, and hard to cure. Modern science has developed a new testing technique, but it is rather unpleasant. Try to avoid catching bilharzia by purifying drinking water.

In Asia all water should be purified since hepatitis is a widespread, easily-transmitted and unpleasant illness.

In Africa there are also soda lakes, containing sodium salts. Usually this water is undrinkable; when you swallow it your throat burns and you vomit. In the dry season when little fresh water enters the lakes, the soda-level is at its worst, but in the rainy season or when the water level rises, the soda may be fairly mild.

I remember arriving at Lake Rudolph which is a soda lake after we'd been walking for weeks in the desert on our way north to Ethiopia. As we came over a big sand-dune we found ourselves on the edge of a vast lake. Mile upon mile of sparkling clear water—seemingly jade coloured, it stretched to faraway purple horizons, and was dotted with extinct volcano islands. I felt stunned.

Gentle white foaming waves tumbled along the sandy beach at our feet. Without stopping to take off my clothes I plunged into the water; it felt unimaginably good. My desert-pony had also rushed eagerly into the water. He lowered his head and drank thirstily. After a few gulps he stopped, looked disappointed, but he drank some more. So I tasted the water. It was alkaline, it burnt my throat slightly and didn't taste nice. But it could have been worse; the pony could drink it and, if necessary, so could I. As for the camel, he wasn't due to drink again for another week, and the fresh-water 5 gallon cans he carried for me were not yet empty.

We wandered for many days along this golden sandy shore, frequently pausing while I dived into the waves and soaked my clothes, since I'd discovered that wearing wet clothes in a hot breeze made me feel wonderfully cool.

To Purify Water

Water that is suspect or impure should be boiled before drinking. It is not enough merely to bring it to the boil, it must boil for at least three minutes.

Otherwise you can use purifying tablets. Puritabs are quick-acting (20 minutes), while Halazone (Sterotabs) act more slowly. Iodine also purifies: 2–4 drops of 7% strength per 1¾ pint (1 litre) of water, and let it stand for 30 minutes before drinking. The taste is not very pleasant, though it can be disguised with fruitjuice powder, or in tea. Be vigilant, but use your commonsense about purifying water. You can overdo it.

I've never suffered a stomach upset from drinking bad water, which is probably due to the good advice of my first travelling companion. She taught me that it is important to build up a resistance to germs. By always sterilising your drinking water you will never develop resistance. By using your judgment, drinking naturally good water (wells and springs, etc.) and working up to being able to drink where tribespeople drink, your body should learn to deal with mild impurities. This resistance is slowly obtained, but worthwhile to long-term campers. However, it does not mean you would withstand strong germs, or that you may freely drink any type of water. Where bilharzia or hepatitis are endemic, better safe than sorry.

Other Sources of Water

Where streams or lakes are unavailable and there is no rainfall, you can still procure yourself a water supply.

Dew is an excellent source of water, best collected after cold clear nights. Drag a cloth through the grass then wring it out. Large glossy leaves attract dew, as do big smooth stones.

Sea water is of course undrinkable, but if you dig a hole just above the high tide line you should find drinkable water. It will taste brackish, but the sand should have filtered out most of the salt; and since salt water is heavier than fresh, the fresh water will be on top. Usually 20 in (½ m) is deep enough. If the hole is too deep the water gets salty.

With a Space Blanket or a sheet of plastic it is not difficult to create condensation. In a low-lying sunny place dig a circular pit, 3 ft (1 m) across and at least 20 in (½ m) deep. Put an empty cookpot at the bottom, and put the plastic (or Space Blanket shiny side down) over the top of the hole. Anchor it firmly around the edges, and weight it down in the centre with a heavy stone, so that the condensation which forms on the underside of the plastic will trickle down and drip into the cookpot. Make sure that the plastic does not touch the sides of the pit or the pot.

This system works best in hot sun, and can produce several pints of water per day, but don't keep lifting up the plastic to look, since this destroys the build-up of moist air. However, you will occasionally need to empty the container, and if you notice that condensation has slowed down a lot, move the whole thing to another spot.

If you put some green leafy plants in the pit (not

touching the plastic) they will hasten the process of condensation. Sea water or polluted water will also speed up the process. Pour the undrinkable water on the ground under the plastic. The 'still' works by vapourising water from the ground, so by putting more moisture there the process becomes more effective. Condensation is pure water vapour, and any impurities are left in the ground.

Many plants store water. In hot climates you may see the distinctive travellers' palm and the travellers' tree (*Ravenala madagascarienses*); in both these trees the bottom of each leaf-stem has a cavity holding about 1¾ pints (1 litre) of water. Just pierce a hole into one and clean water will gush out. The fountain tree of tropical Asia contains drinkable sap in its main stem, and the water tree of tropical Africa contains good water in its climbing branches.

Woody vines such as rattans and wild grapevines often store water. Cut off a vine high up, then cut it off again at the base, and put the end in a container. The watery sap drains out. When it seems finished, cut it shorter on top to allow more sap to flow out. Every time you shorten it the pressure releases more liquid.

Succulent juices may be obtained from the buds of coconut and cabbage palms; and trees such as the maple and birch may be tapped for their plentiful sap. Cut a V-shaped groove and put a splinter of wood in the bottom for liquid to run outwards.

Cactus plants (such as the prickly pear, giant cactus and the barrel cactus which earns the name 'water barrel') contain watery juice which may be squeezed out. Burn off the thorns and cut a hole in the top before you start squeezing.

7   Building an Open Fire

Where to Position your Fire

The position of your fire is important since you don't want to be sitting in its smoke. Check the wind direction. Bear in mind that it may veer and change direction, and that even a still day can become gusty.

It is wise to make a fire somewhere sheltered by rocks or on the leeside of a big damp log.

In dry conditions remember that the fire should not be within spitting distance of dry grass and undergrowth.

If you do not want to leave any traces of having camped or made fire, find a green-grassy nook and remove the turf. Cut the turf to the depth of its roots and roll it back. Use the space for the fire. If you stay several days, you should water the roll of turf. When you leave, re-fit the turf in the hole; no trace of the fire will show.

Firewood

Looking around for firewood is something I enjoy; it gives me the chance to explore in detail the area of my camp and see where I am. Firewood should be dead and dry. Do not use green living wood and don't use rotten-crumbly dead wood since it won't burn. If wood feels cold to touch, it's probably damp; not ideal for a young fire, but all right for slowing down a hot one. Dry driftwood on beaches and riverbanks is generally excellent firewood. Fallen trees provide root-wood, which burns slowly, gives a lot of heat, and is usually smokeless.

There are certain types of wood that refuse to burn well, even when dry; they just smoulder and are useless. These include alder, chestnut, elder, elm, poplar, and willow. Others, such as pine and blackthorn, are notorious for the way they spit and spark. Bamboo, if not split open, will explode with a noise like gunshot.

For wood that burns fast and furious try birch, hazel, holly, fir trees, and softwoods in general. These are good for feeding a young fire, and for boiling a pot of water quickly. However, softwoods burn to ash without producing the red-hot embers that you need for serious cooking.

For a longer-lasting slower fire with plenty of red embers, use wood such as ash, beech, birch, maple, oak and other hardwoods.

When you cook meat over a fire, you will find that the taste of the meat is affected by the type of wood used. Don't use coniferous wood (such as pine) since it is too resinous which gives an overpowering taste. Good flavours are obtained from oak, sycamore or beech. Superb flavours are given by apple, cherry and pear wood; only a few sticks are necessary, added towards the end of the meat's cooking time. Try and find, too, a few sprigs of juniper, bay or fennel (good with fish); again, add at the end of the cooking time.

Try playing with smoke-flavours, blending them and just enjoying the smells.

Substitutes for Firewood

Where there's no firewood, people find substitutes such as peat, or dry cattle dung. The dung doesn't smell bad because it is only processed grass, without chemicals. If the cattle eat chemical products, it makes a difference to the smell. Beware if you have skin cuts or scratches, since dung is known to carry tetanus. Dry seaweed makes a hot but not a spectacular fire. Bones can also be used, as Charles Darwin discovered. Use fresh or old bones. The size of the flames will depend on the amount of fat in the bones.

Kindling

To start a fire you will need some kindling. Use things such as dry grass, dry leaves (especially holly), dead gorse, old birds' nests, newspaper, or strips of bark from the silver birch or paper trees (thin strips make ideal kindling and will also burn when wet). Mix these with very small brittle-dry dead twigs. The best twigs come from beech or coniferous trees.

In wet weather look for kindling under bushes and below the top layer in piles of fallen leaves (but be alert for snakes). Or knock the bark off damp dead branches and use your knife to slice slivers off the dry wood. Provided you have matches or a lighter, you can use kindling to start off a fire. If you've run out or got them wet then you need to do a bit more work.

Tinder

Tinder is smaller and dryer than kindling, and is needed to produce fire from an original spark. Use the fluffy lining of an old birds' nest, or kapok, any dry fluff (eg. bulrush), stray bits of sheep's wool, or cotton rag-cloth (cotton rope is good). Otherwise, try crumbled dead ferns, lichen, pine needles, or the dried fibrous inner bark of coniferous trees.

To Create an Original Spark

In remote corners of the world there are many people who live without matches and lighters. Usually they keep a fire permanently going, letting it die down in the day and reviving it when required. If the fire goes out, they just fetch some hot embers from their neighbours. However, spark-creating tools are often kept handy, and many times on hunting expeditions I've seen them used. Methods vary according to what is locally available. Most recently I saw a man using a stick of hardwood, split at one end with a stone placed in the split to hold it open. Into the gap he put very dry crumbled tinder, and he looped a string (of bush-fibre) round the split stick. It lay slightly raised off the ground, held firm by his foot, and he began to pull the two ends of the string rapidly to and fro. The friction of the string on the wood produced enough heat to make the tinder smoulder, and the man blew the fire gently into life.

Other methods employ two flint-type stones, one of which is usually cracked open in a previous fire to get a sharp side. An easier method is to use stone and metal. The stone must be flint, or any siliceous stone such as quartz, agate or obsidian. The metal must be steel or hardened iron. Try using your knife.

Hold the flint just above a small pile of tinder, and strike the metal downwards against it (or vice versa). Keep trying; a spark should eventually fall into the tinder and start to smoulder. When smouldering, pick it up and blow it gently into flame.

A method for modern travellers is to use a camera lens. You will need to open the back of the camera (having rewound the film), and set the aperture on its, widest reading. Let the sun's rays shine straight into the open back and out of the lens, on to the tinder.

Don't let me give you the impression that any of these methods is easy—it's not. But in an emergency you've nothing to lose by trying.

Building a Fire
Making fires burn seems easy, until you try. I'm surprised how many people go about it the wrong way, and are baffled when the fire fails.

Even after a rainstorm it is usually possible to coax a fire into existence. In damp conditions you will need more kindling. So long as you can get the fire started, it won't matter if wood is damp—it'll dry in the fire. Use thin wood or split pieces since they dry much faster than thick pieces. And knock the bark off them.

If the ground is damp, lay the fire on a base of parallel sticks.

The craft of fire lighting lies in the way you arrange the wood. Put the kindling in a very loose pile, and use a few thin dry sticks to make a pyramid-shape over it. Don't use many sticks, the fire needs plenty of airspace. Light the kindling, and as the flames creep up on to the sticks add more dry sticks one by one into the area where the flames are greatest. Keep the fire loosely contained, don't smother it; allow the flames to take hold. Gradually add bigger firewood to the pyramid shape.

If the fire begins to die, probably there is too much wood and not enough air-draught. Blow slowly on the smouldering bits to revive them and add some kindling. Should you blow too violently, you will blow the fire out. If the fire fails completely, take the whole pile apart and start again. Have patience, talk to the fire and feed it twig by twig.

Once the fire is going, it will take about half an hour before it is hot enough to cook a proper meal, so allow sufficient time. The ideal fire for cooking food is a mass of red embers. After burning strongly for ten minutes the fire can be rearranged to the most appropriate shape for your requirements. When cooking at mountain altitudes, remember the boiling-point of water is much lower than at sealevel. The food might be boiling, without being hot enough actually to cook. In such conditions it can take half an hour to cook an egg.

Fire Shapes and Types
The pyramid shape with near-vertical sticks gives the fastest-burning type of fire, and is suitable for quick boiling, toasting, or baking in hot ashes.

The flatter you lay the sticks, the slower the fire will burn. For a good slow-burning effect put thicker wood horizontally in criss-crossing layers. This will produce plentiful red embers for grilling or roasting, and a flat surface for the cookpot.

When firewood is very scarce it is best to make a star-shaped fire, with a few big logs placed flat on the ground like spokes radiating from the hub of embers. Push the logs in as they burn up. Pots can be balanced on their meeting point.

A *rock-fire*—is built leaning against a sheer-faced rock (ideally flat-topped for a working-surface). The rock will absorb and reflect the fire's heat, which speeds up the roasting of food and continues to radiate warmth all night. It is a marvellous fire in cold weather.

In cold places if no big rock is available, I suggest you gather the largest stones you can find, but not flints or wet riverbed stones, which tend to crack or explode when heated. Use them to build a semi-circular wall round the back of the fire to produce reflected heat.

A trench fire—is good for windy days or when firewood is scarce. Dig a small sloping trench in line with the wind. The back end should be less than 20 in (½ m) deep, and narrow enough to support cookpots. The front end should be more open and slope up to ground-level. Make the fire in the deep end; you can feed it with long branches, just push them further in as they burn up. Very convenient for long simmering or stewing.

If you intend staying several days it is worth lining the trench with stones. Stones will help conserve heat, the fire will require less fuel during cooking, and the stones will also stop the trench sides from crumbling in to collapse, though clay works well without stones.

A hunter's fire—stops a fire smoking. Place logs or rocks in a funnel shape, the wide end facing into the breeze. Put some thinnish dry firewood at the narrow end. Make it catch fire, and the flames should negate the smoke. When made in a wider V-shape the hunter's fire can serve a double purpose: push the hot embers to the back for cooking, and have a flaming fire at the mouth for warmth and quick boiling.

Words of Warning
It is illegal in some places to light fires unless you get permission from the landowner. Gathering firewood on private land also needs permission.

Don't make the fire too large, as large fires are harder to

control. Should it get out of control, stamp out the sparks with your feet, throw water on flaming grass, or beat out the flames with a broom of whippy twigs. Or else throw earth or sand on the flames; smother them and they will die.

If your clothes catch fire, roll on the ground or in water, or smother the flames with a blanket or sleeping bag. The best first aid for fire burns is immersion in cold water.

Should the wind begin to gust, build up around your fire with logs and rocks. Never leave a fire unattended.

When you get smoke in your eyes don't rub them, it merely aggravates the problem. Scoop up a handful of clean water and hold it to each eye, opening the eye underwater.

An understanding of fires is something for which one may be eternally grateful. There are many times when I've been wet and miserably cold, but then been warmed, dried out and comforted by a fire. Late one afternoon in the barren mountains of Lesotho, the sky became overcast with dark-greenish clouds, which brought torrential rain and a hailstorm.

I urged my horse into the shelter of some fern trees but the hailstones smashed the fern branches and we were left exposed. The hailstones were as big and hard as golfballs, very painful, and rivulets of icy water poured down my neck.

The sky grew darker again, and in anguish I began searching a rocky outcrop for good shelter. Round the back there was a boulder-cave spacious enough to accommodate both the horse and me. We crept inside, shivering and utterly miserable.

In one corner the wind had collected a pile of dry ferny kindling. I used it to start the fire, then added a damp fern tree trunk. The wood was terribly smoky but the wind pushed the smoke away. I hung my clothes to dry and put a billycan of water to boil for tea.

Outside the cave, the storm was awe-inspiring. And

inside, as my eyes adjusted to the dimness, I noticed that the largest surfaces of the boulders which created the cave were decorated with primitive ochre shapes of men and beasts, the paintings of a bushman.

I sat by the fire, enjoying the warmth, sipping tea, and feeling absurdly contented.

8   Campsite Housekeeping

Ground Ovens

Ground ovens or fire pits are traditional methods of cooking in various ethnic groups and ideal when you want to be able to ignore your cooking or go away for the day without leaving an open fire or creating cooking smells. The size of the pit should be just a bit larger than what you intend cooking, allowing room all round for hot embers. A shallow hole would suit a fish, but a sheep would need a pit 3 ft (1 m) deep. Let's assume you want to cook a big chicken. Dig a hole about 20 in ($\frac{1}{2}$ m) deep and 20 in ($\frac{1}{2}$ m) wide. Line the bottom (and sides, if you like) with large stones (not flints). Don't worry if you can't find any stones; in short-term cooking they're helpful but not vital.

Build a fire in the hole and make it burn fiercely until the ground feels warm and there are plenty of hot embers. This takes at least an hour. Push the embers to the pit sides and remove a pile of embers and hot rocks, using two flat bits of wood as tongs.

Wrap your chicken in a thick layer of damp leaves or clay.

Clay, or cloying mud, is highly suitable for cooking whole birds, small game, porcupine and hedgehog. Dry clay must be kneaded with water until it is soft and flexible. Flatten it into a sheet about an inch thick, then roll the food in it, add some root vegetables or mushrooms, before pinching the ends shut.

Most animals should be gutted before cooking (see Chapter 10). Don't bother plucking a bird, since its feathers will stick to the clay and after cooking when you rip off the clay mould the feathers come away with it. The same goes for the quills of porcupine or hedgehog.

Put the package into the pit and fill the space round

and above it with the hot rocks and embers. If you want to hasten the cooking, light a fire on top of the pit. Otherwise, place some large leaves (banana leaves are best) over the top to hold in the steam. Cover the top of the pit with earth.

The food inside will cook slowly, retaining its succulence and flavour, and should be ready three to five hours later. It cannot get overcooked since the heat is continually fading, but it should keep warm for about twenty-four hours.

Usually a ground oven works terribly well, but of course the silliest things can go wrong. As I returned to my camp after a long day's climbing in the hills, I congratulated myself on having left a guinea-fowl cooking in a ground oven; it would be ready to eat and I was very hungry.

I had slight trouble locating my camp because I'd hidden my gear under bushes and cleared away all signs of my presence; but soon I recognised some landmarks, and re-established the camp. Picking up the shovel-stick I'd used to dig the oven I realised that I couldn't remember where it was. I'd been so thorough about removing traces that there was nothing to give me a clue. In an effort to detect the hot ground above the oven I crawled around on my hands and knees, but the stony sand was hot everywhere from the afternoon sun. The position was so ridiculous that I began to laugh.

Test diggings yielded nothing. I became increasingly puzzled, frustrated and hungry—and worried that perhaps I'd merely imagined making the oven. Muttering 'perseverance must pay off' I dug in lines like a huge game of 'Battleships'. It was sunset before I hit lucky. However, the guinea-fowl tasted so good that I forgave myself.

The moral of this tale is, when hiding an oven, mark the spot.

Foiled Again and Again

Heavy duty kitchen tinfoil is an infinitely practical thing to carry with you. It can be wrapped around food to bake in hot embers or ash, or used to improvise a saucepan or a frying pan, or as an oven for baking bread.

To cook meat (chops, chunks, slices, joints) or fish in foil, grease the shiny side of the foil. Put the meat on the foil, season and add onions and any other vegetables. Close the foil to make a parcel, allowing some airspace for the heat to circulate, and pinch the joins tightly shut. You could add a little stock, or wine, cider or some sauce to make it extra delicious.

The parcel can be buried to cook in ashes and embers, or put to sit on top of the embers (best if they're not red-hot). Shake or turn the parcel occasionally.

Tinfoil adapts to cup-shape (moulded over a cup or your fist), and may be used to heat water for tea, and to boil or poach an egg. Small amounts of stew could be heated the same way.

An improvised frying pan may be made from tinfoil wrapped over the V-shaped end of a forked green stick. Push the foil down to make a dent. Grease it for frying.

If you have a grill-wire, put a flat bit of foil on it for frying fish (which tends to fall apart as it cooks), and for open-frying small things such as mushrooms, eggs and onions.

Potatoes and other tubers are excellent when baked in foil. Grease the skin first. A big potato takes nearly an hour to cook in the embers.

You can improvise a reflecting oven with tinfoil. Make it with a shiny tin box, like a biscuit tin, or with foil folded into a box-shape, shiny side inwards, joints pinched tightly shut, and propped into shape by green sticks. The box must be open at one side, and should be the same height and width as the fire. The food needs to be raised off the bottom, ideally at mid-height, resting on a wire mesh or something similar.

Light a fire about a foot outside the open mouth of the box, and make a wind-shelter of logs or stones curving round behind the fire so that much heat will be reflected into the box. The box should have its back to the breeze.

If the fire is kept blazing hot, the oven will be adequate

for baking bread (see Chapter 9) or for roasting big joints of meat. There is no problem about burning the food since you can see into the oven at a glance. If the food is getting over-brown, move the box a bit further away from the fire.

Sticks and Stones

Bakestones—a large flat stone will serve as a bakestone for baking cookies and unleavened bread, and may also be used for frying on, or as a warming plate. Don't use flints or wet riverbed stones.

Put the stone into the fire, and heat it until it is so hot that water dripped on it sizzles into vapour. A frying-pan-sized slab of stone will take about half an hour to reach this heat, then push the stone to the side of the fire for use. It will stay baking hot for about half an hour more. Bigger stones take longer to heat and retain baking heat for longer periods. If the stone is too heavy to move, build a fire over it, then remove the fire.

Grease the top of a bakestone before cooking on it.

Another use of hot stones is for warming water for washing and doing the pots. Just heat some stones and drop them in a bowl of cold water.

Skewers—Long before man had metal or saucepans, he used sticks to hold his food during cooking, for toasting, skewering, spit-roasting.

Avoid using sticks from coniferous trees (pine, etc.) since the resin affects the food's flavour, and also the wood from nut-bearing trees, which gives food a bitter taste. Use green sticks (cut from a living tree), peel them, and soak the end of the stick in water before use.

Food may be speared and toasted by flames, or supported above the fire on two parallel raised sticks, or spitted on a raised cross-pole. Meat and firm vegetables can also be cooked in this way. Skewered fruit is especially delicious if toasted on kebabs and basted with something syrupy, which crystallises on the fruit as it cooks (see Chapter 15).

If you've got better things to do than sit holding a stick over a fire, then push one end into the ground, or anchor it with a rock, and slant the stick over the fire, propped up halfway along by a forked stick. Turn the cooking-stick occasionally so the food is evenly browned.

Griddles and Barbecues

A serviceable griddle may be produced from an old piece of sheet metal or a sawn-off upturned oildrum. The sawn-off oildrum should stand about a foot high and have a wide opening in the side to let the fire breathe. Build the fire inside.

A scrap of wire-mesh or a metal grid could enable you to barbecue food with great ease. Some campers carry a grill-wire for this purpose, and it is also useful for standing pots upright. Steaks, kebabs, and vegetables grilled on a barbecue taste superb.

A Bamboo Cookpot

While trekking in the bamboo jungles of Thailand's Golden Triangle, my companion (a nine-year-old Burmese boy) taught me to cook food inside a bamboo. This is not the thin meagre bamboo that grows in cool climates; in the tropics its stems can be as wide as saucers, and so tall they soar up into high cathedral vaulting archways. Bamboo is an invaluable plant in those regions, used by the hill tribes for making almost everything they need.

Medium-fat bamboo stems are good as temporary cookpots. Cut 1½ segments of bamboo; the extra half will protect the woody partition from extreme heat, leaving only the top end open. Food must be cooked in water or liquid to prevent the bamboo burning. Angle the bamboo over the fire, heat stew in it, or simmer vegetables. For steaming you should plug the top with a wedge of leaves. Bamboo cookpots give a delicious flavour to food cooked in them.

Slimmer bamboo is perfect for the overnight making of porridge or rice-sticks. Every night before sleeping we'd fill a couple of bamboo tubes with rice and water, a pinch of salt (and sometimes some chopped nuts) then seal the top with a bung of leaves, and push it at a slant into the fire's warm ashes.

In the morning we simply had to strip away the bamboo (like peeling sugarcane) to expose a solid tube of superbly-flavoured rice. Only peel the amount you want to eat, the rest stays neatly packed in the stem, excellent for occasional bites and mid-day snacks. It's sustaining, and ideal for trekkers and campers in general.

A Hide Cookpot
Another way to improvise a container for cooking liquid is by using the hide of an animal. Suspend the hide above the fire, from a branch or supports, and so long as there is plenty of liquid in the hide it will not burn through.

Safe and Cool
When intending to camp in one spot for a while it could be worth making a food safe, to protect food from birds and flying insects. A safe is easily improvised with a

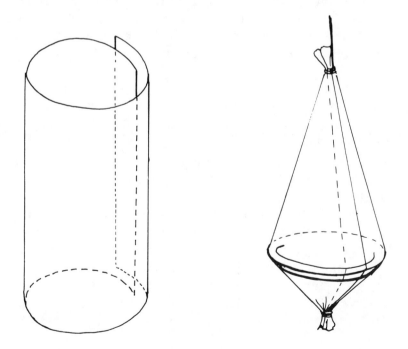

length of muslin and some string. Fold the muslin to make a tube, with sides overlapping but not stitched. Tie the top and bottom shut with string. Hang it from a shady tree. Pull open the overlap to put a plate of food inside.

To prevent ants climbing down the string, try smearing it with grease.

To combat sugar ants in the tropics, people's food safes stand on legs in dishes of water, because ants can't swim.

To keep things cool—immerse them in a cold running stream. Use a watertight container and anchor it firmly on the streambed with rocks. In a deep cold river, put the container in a plastic bag, weighted with stones, and fasten to a rock or root on the bank. Watch out for big fish!

Or wrap a container in a wet cloth and hang it from a shady tree, exposed to the breeze. The cloth will need re-damping every now and again.

To keep a bottle of milk fresh, stand it in the shade in a dish of water, and cover it with a damp cloth whose edges are in the water. If put in the breeze this works very well. But on thundery days milk always seems to go sour.

A haybox, insulated bag, or food-flask will keep food cool, provided the food was cold when you put it in.

Doing the Pots
To clean the black soot off your cooking-pots, sprinkle them with ash from the fire or with sand, and take a handful of wet grass to use as a scrubber.

To prevent your pots getting blackened by the fire, rub some soap on the outside before you begin cooking. After cooking, just wash the soap and soot off.

To make washing-up easier, put water in the cookpots straight after you've finished with them. Use cold water for porridge pots and floury or eggy things, and hot water for greasy ones.

To clean the inside of dirty cookpots, improvise a pot-scourer by using a handful of wiry grass, or leaves, heather, horsetail (pewterwort), or other springy and abrasive plants. If you add some sand to your improvised scourer it will work wonders. Sand is excellent for washing-up; it can be used instead of soap.

Frying pans should not be washed, just wipe them clean with some leaves or grass.

Bottles may be cleaned by putting some sand and water inside, then shaking the bottle thoroughly.

9 Baking

When you wander into remote regions you are unlikely to find bread for sale. Of course, bread is not essential to survival, but it is useful for mid-day snacks; and there's nothing quite like the taste of fresh hot bread.

Any type of improvised oven (see Chapter 8) will do, or you can simply put extra flour on the outside of the loaf and bury it to bake in hot ashes.

Bread
Bread-baking doesn't have to be tedious and difficult, nor does bread have to look like a baker's loaf. Mine usually look terrible but taste fine. There can be endless variations on the basic theme. Whatever ingredients you haven't got, either leave them out or substitute something similar.

The heavier the ingredients, the slower they should be cooked. To find out whether bread is ready to eat, slide a knife blade into the loaf; if dough sticks to it, it is not yet cooked. When the knife comes out clean, the bread is ready.

Using yeast the basic theme is:

1 big mug of flour	1 tsp sugar
½ packet of dried yeast	½ tsp salt
½ mug of water	

Put the yeast, sugar and water to soak for half an hour. It will produce a thick grey foam when it is ready to be used. Put the flour in a billycan, add the salt, and make a well in the centre for pouring the liquid into when ready.

Pour in the liquid, slowly, stirring well. Cover the billycan with a lid and leave it in a warm undraughty place for 15 minutes. It reacts best at about 80°F (26.6°C), but better too cool than too hot. If it's too warm the yeast dies. When risen, knead it with your hands, and leave it to rise again, for about 30 minutes. Then bake it for an hour in an oven or ashes.

If you're using a bakestone instead, the dough should be an inch thick. Let it rise once for 15 minutes, and bake it on a medium-hot stone for 20 minutes each side. The bread won't rise as much as in an oven.

Bread-baking without yeast— If you don't have yeast, you can make light fluffy bread with baking powder and self-raising flour.

Self-raising flour is simple to use: just mix it with a pinch of salt and enough water to make a stiff dough. Then pat it to 1 in (2½ cm) thick and cook it on a bakestone for 10 minutes each side.

The taste improves if you use milk instead of water, or add a beaten egg and some butter or fat. Mix the egg and butter with the flour before adding the milk, and let it stand for an hour before baking.

It's good with raisins, nuts and spices especially nutmeg and cinnamon.

Bicarbonate of soda has the same rising effect as baking powder but it makes your tongue tingle and is an acquired taste. If you don't like it, try adding cream of tartar.

Using baking powder (or bicarbonate of soda and cream of tartar mixed 1:2¼) to make bread:

2 mugs of flour	2 tsp baking powder
¾ mug of water (or milk)	1 tsp salt (optional)

Mix all the dry ingredients. If milk means milk powder, add it to the dry things. Sieving the flour produces lighter bread.

Make a well in the dry ingredients and pour the water slowly into it, stirring constantly until it is a thick smooth dough. Knead the dough briefly, and immediately put it to bake in fast heat for about 40 minutes. Or divide it into rolls and bake them for 20 minutes. If you delay in putting the mixture to cook, the baking powder loses its raising power.

This type of dough works well in an oven or baked under ashes, or on a bakestone.

Rolls

Rolls are easier to make successfully than bread. Prepare the dough as for bread, but after the first rise divide it into balls. Let it rise again for about 15 minutes, then bake for 30 minutes.

Biscuits

A more biscuit-worthy dough is made from:

2 mugs of flour	2–3 tablespoons of butter,
¾ mug of milk or water	lard or fat
4 tsp baking powder	½ tsp salt

Mix all the dry ingredients and add the shortening (butter/fat) by rubbing it into the dry mixture with your fingers until there are no more lumps. Stir in the milk or water slowly, mixing it thoroughly, to make a thick dough. Flatten the dough out on a piece of greased or floured tinfoil, cover with more tinfoil, and put it to bake for 10–15 minutes. Cut it into squares and eat them hot. But keep some for later to be sprinkled with water and re-heated.

Different biscuits can be made using a mug of flour and a mug of corn-meal, or other types of meal; or by adding chopped nuts, currants, or spices, etc.

Scones

To make scones:

1 mug of flour	½ mug milk or water
1 tsp baking powder	pinch of salt
¼ mug butter or	a little sugar (optional)
margarine (or half that	(lemon powder and
quantity with an egg	chopped raisins are
added)	also good)

Mix (or sieve) the dry ingredients, rub in the butter, add the liquid and stir it all into a soft dough. Divide it into dollops, roll them quickly in flour and bake them for 15 minutes. Sometimes mine turn out more like cookies.

Good with jam or syrup and cream.

Unleavened Bread
Alternatively, make unleavened bread. Without any rising-agent you can bake things such as oatcakes, hardtack, potato scones, semolina cookies and shortbread.

If you don't have any flour either, you could still bake with crushed grain or root vegetables, to make flat cakes and biscuits.

Here are some variations on the baking theme.

Dampers
Instead of going to all the trouble of baking in an oven at the end of a long day, you can just twist the dough round a stick to make a damper. Mix some self-raising flour with just a little water, adding the water slowly and mixing until you have a thick dough. Knead it, and add a pinch of salt, then roll the dough into worms, of ½ in (1 cm) or 1 in (2½ cm) thickness. Dampen a few peeled sticks with water and coil a dough-worm round the end of each stick. Coil it loosely-spaced like a corkscrew for good crust. Put the dough over the heat, cook the curly ends first so they don't unwrap, and turn the stick occasionally until the dampers are golden brown. To test when they are ready, rap the stick. The damper slides off when it is done. Very nice for a snack with chocolate.

Sour dough
This is the traditional frontiersman bread, but you have to wait forty-eight hours while it ferments. Use:

2 mugs of flour	2 tablespoons of sugar
2 mugs of warm water	1 tsp salt

Mix the dry ingredients in a pot and stir in enough water to make a slightly sloppy dough. Cover the pot and leave it in a warm place (about 90°F or 32.2°C) to ferment for 48 hours. It should double in size. Don't worry about the smell, it will go away in the baking.

To make sour-dough bread, add a spoon of melted fat and as much flour as the sloppy dough will absorb to make it thick like ordinary bread-dough. If you add a teaspoon of bicarbonate of soda it will neutralise the sour taste of the bread. Knead the dough a little, place it then in a greased dish or in dollops on tinfoil and leave in a warm place to rise again for an hour for a loaf or 15 minutes for dollops. When risen, bake it in medium heat until cooked.

To make more, keep back a mugful of the fermented sloppy dough, and later add more water and flour to it. It only needs about 12 hours for fermentation.

Sour-dough is also good with added dried milk and dried egg, and baked on a bakestone. In the tropics palm wine may be used instead of water.

Hardtack
This is made with the same ingredients as sour-dough, but is different in proportion, method and taste.

Hardtack is ideal for hikers as it is very compact and will keep well for many months. But it tends to get so hard that you have to dip it in tea, coffee or soup before you can eat it.

To make hardtack:

2 mugs of flour	½ tsp sugar
½ tsp salt	some water

Mix the dry ingredients with just enough water to make a stiff dough. Knead it well, then pat it into a thin sheet and cut it into squares. Put the squares on to greased or floured tinfoil or a bakestone and bake them for about 20 minutes, until brittle dry.

Using the same basic recipe with a drop more water, and any other ingredients you fancy, you should be able to turn out some excellent cookies. Bake until cooked (test with knife) not until dry.

While I was prospecting for gold with a couple of Afrikaaner gypsies in the mountains of South Africa, I lived on hardtack. The old gipsy woman spoke no

English, so I let her teach me some cookery. She showed me how to make hardtack, and it became my staple diet. Somehow it matched the dry crumbly sun-scorched countryside where we walked.

After leaving the gypsies I continued with my horse along the old gold-mining belt which curves down South Africa. One day at noon I rode into a ghost town on a rocky hilltop.

I had a weird kind of picnic in the middle of the ghost town, with hardtack and biltong (dried meat), and coffee to wash it down, sharing the hardtack with the horse.

Improvised Bread

At the simplest end of the scale, oatcakes can be made from oatmeal and water. (If you have salt, add a pinch.) Use enough water to make the meal into a stiff dough, and bake it until lightly browned.

If you have fat, melt it and use it as well as, or instead of water. Rub the fat into the meal with your fingers to make a dough. Knead it and divide it into flat dollops. Prick them with a fork and bake them on a greased bakestone for 10 minutes each side. Then coat the oatcakes in dry meal and roast them on the fire until crisp.

Cakes may also be made out of potatoes or any starchy root vegetable or tuber (eg. carrot, turnip, cassava, yam etc.).

For simple cakes the tubers can be cooked and mashed in advance, or just coarsely grated raw. Whichever way, mix them with a dab of melted butter or fat, and some flour or dried egg to bind them together. Add salt and pepper, and enough water or milk to make it dough-like. Divide into flat rounds, sprinkle them with flour, prick them with a fork, and fry them in a pan until brown on both sides (about 15 minutes). Eat them hot, cut open and spread with butter.

My best recollection of improvising bread was in a desert. My provisions were meagre, but I did have some maize meal and a few odds and ends of other things. Wandering along we met a camel herdsman. I wouldn't have stopped but my camel got surrounded by his camels, and when he came over to sort them out, I noticed that he was carrying a gourd full of fresh camel milk. We talked in mime, and he agreed to swop some milk for some chewing tobacco, which he stuck inside his ornate bone lip-plug, and we parted. Stony desert mountains lay all around. I decided to camp since we had reached a shallow valley with some grazing for my two animals and dead wood for a fire.

I unloaded the horse and camel, made camp, collected firewood and built a fire in a stony hole. While the fire gained heat I mixed a dough of maize flour, chopped root of ginger, saccharine, baking powder, salt, and camel milk, which is thickish and sweet. To avoid the necessity of washing-up (no spare water) I'd line the billycan with foil, and just buried the pot in the fire's embers.

Half an hour later it was perfectly cooked and as I put it aside to cool, I saw the camel-man returning. He wasn't alone, but had brought his friends. I felt uneasy. They sat down near my camp, but then I realised they weren't watching me, they were entranced by the horse. One man stood up, went over to the horse, and in a high nasal voice he sang to it.

Standing there in that stony lunar desert, his red-ochred body contrasting against the purple-coloured rocks and mauve-ish tongues of ancient lava, he sang his strange falsetto song.

From his companions I learnt that they had never seen a horse in this part of the world, and the song was in reverence. The men had brought me another gourd of camel milk, and a hunk of dried camel meat. Then we all shared my gingerbread, which was excellent, and we finished the lot.

Baking can be a wonderful thing.

Substitutes for Bread – Without Baking
This seems to be an appropriate place to mention certain plants that produce bread-substitutes.

In temperate climates, the Tartar bread plant of Eastern Europe and Asia has a thick fleshy root which can be sliced and eaten raw. (Julius Caesar's soldiers are noted to have used it.) And the Kaffir bread tree of Southern Africa has an edible stem which is made into bread.

In the tropics, the breadfruit tree (*Antrocarpus incisa*) grows in all hot wet climates and gives a generous supply of nutritious bread. The thick white layer inside the immature fruit tastes like fresh bread. It must be cooked (roasted/baked/boiled/fried) before being eaten. The breadnut tree (*Brosium alicastrum*) yields fruit which, when cooked, is used as bread. The gingerbread tree (*Hyphaene thebaica*) of tropical Africa has big clusters of fruit whose mealy husks taste like gingerbread.

10   *Preparation of Game*

The quality of meat is governed by the type and age of the animal, and by the time of year. Most wild meats are at their best around the end of the summer or wet season, when the animals have put on weight to last them through the cold or dry months ahead.

There is no animal whose meat is naturally poisonous, though certain parts of their offal may be—the acid enzymes of a crocodile's stomach are strong enough to dissolve bones. But remember, meat is made from what the animal eats; carnivores taste different from herbivores, and those that scavenge are not good-tasting. No one eats vultures. (But they do eat crows—in parts of the USA farmers hold crow-banquets.)

What farmers and landowners would class as vermin (rabbits, squirrels, pigeons, etc.) are free for hunting at any time of year, though on private land you need the landowner's permission to be there. Game hunting usually requires a licence and most animals are protected by law during their breeding season.

If you should find an animal freshly-dead from natural causes—well—a bushman in Africa would sit down, build a fire, cook and eat his fill, then take away as much as he could carry. But let me quote a timely warning from an earlier traveller: beware the animal that has lain dead a few hours in hot sun. The heat of the sun forms gases in the stomach. If you must cut, approach cautiously, take care not to come from the leeward and check your retreat is clear. Reaching arm full length, drive spear into abdomen, leaping backward at same time to avoid gaseous and liquid explosion.

What To Do With the Body
Professional butchering of large animals is a matter of

skill, which one doesn't hope to master by reading a couple of pages, but it is helpful to know the right way to go about it when one's a long way from the nearest expert.

Of course you can just hack the carcase to bits, but by cutting down where you should have cut across, you will ruin the quality of the meat, making it tough and fibrous instead of tender. Cleaning and preparing a bullock-sized weight of dead meat is a task that shouldn't be lightly undertaken, and it is certainly not worthwhile unless you're in a large hungry group. Using 8 oz (225 g) portions a carcase of beef will feed fifty people for a week. However, if you should have reason to try your hand at it, this is how it is done.

Don't leave the dead animal lying in the sun. It should be bled and gutted soon after death. To bleed it, sever the four large bloodvessels in the neck. As soon as these jugular vessels are cut, blood gushes everywhere and the dead animal may kick in convulsive spasms. Actually I'm a bit squeamish about blood, and have been known to faint at the sight of it—though not when it is important!

Gutting a bullock can be done with the bullock lying on sloping ground, with its legs pointing downhill, or by hanging the body from a tree (loop a rope over a strong branch). You don't need to hoist the body into mid-air, just up enough to help your work. Hanging it by the head is good if you want to keep and preserve the skin, and all right for drainage; but for bleeding it is better to chop off the head and hang the body upside-down.

Use a sharp knife to slit the skin over the belly, taking care not to puncture through the lining into the entrails. Put your finger as a guard under the knifepoint. Slit the belly skin from the chestbone over the belly and up between the hind legs. Stop cutting just before the anus. Then cut a circle around this, pull it out and tie string tightly round it (to prevent muck spewing out during cleaning).

The next task is to skin the belly area. Grasp an edge

of skin and pull it outwards with one hand, using your other hand to ease the hide away from its lining. Having finished skinning the belly, cut a full-length slit in the abdominal lining (again with your finger guarding the knifepoint). Cut away the genitals, remove the caul fat and anything else that holds the guts in place. When the guts are free, they will come sliding out. Split the breast-bone (with a machete) to remove the heart, lungs, etc.

If you are not planning to dissect the carcase immedi-ately, leave the skin on it. Just prop its chest cavity open with sticks and arrange your mosquito-net so that no flies can get at the carcase. Where the temperature is below 50°F (10°C), it is traditional to hang the carcase (upside-down) for a week or two before eating any meat, as hanging improves the flavour and makes the meat more tender. In cool climates hang it for at least a day, since very fresh meat is particularly tough. The liver and kidneys are the only parts which are best eaten fresh. But don't try hanging a carcase in the tropics.

Skinning is easiest done immediately after gutting, before the body is stone cold. Slit the hide round the animal's neck, and down the throat between the front legs to the belly-slit. Where the skin is soft it can be peeled off with your hands, but tough hide needs a knife for stroking the skin away from the fatty layer beneath it. To skin the legs, cut down the inner sides, and flay them down to the knee-joints.

Sever the lower legs at the joints. Cut off the head if you haven't already done so. Then chop the carcase in open halves, and work out where to make the joint cuts. This is important since meat of muscles which have worked hard needs to be cut across the grain of fibre.

Identifying the Parts
The upper part of the hind legs have several cuts. The meat in front of the bone is called thick flank, and is good for steaks or thick roast beef. The inside leg is topside; cut steaks from it and roast the aitchbone joint. The outside back portion is silverside, suitable for boiling.

The rump is nicest cut into thickish steaks for grilling or roasting. The portion next along the backbone contains the kidneys, sirloin, and fore-ribs. Sirloin is for steaks. Ribs are usually roasted.

At the front end of the body above the backbone is meat known as chuck steak, good for pies or stewing. Between the front legs is the brisket or breast, also used for stewing. At the front of the chest is the clod, suitable for stews or soups.

Also for soups and stews the neck (stickling) is often chosen, as are the shins (of all legs), and any odd bits of meat that aren't good enough for roasting or grilling.

In the tropics, just take what cuts you want to cook and to distribute to other people; the rest of the meat should be cut into strips and hung up to dry into biltong (see the end of this chapter).

In Africa, nothing is wasted. In markets I have seen small squares of cow-hide sold as flavouring for soup.

Further Parts
Here's how to cope with cooking parts of an animal beyond the usual liver and kidneys with which we are most familiar.

Heart—Raw hearts should be thoroughly washed in several changes of water and left soaking in cold water for about an hour. Then drain and dry them. The best methods of cooking are in a stew with vegetables and plenty of thick brown gravy, or stuffed and baked in medium oven-heat for 2–3 hours.

Lungs—These should be beaten with a mallet or flat stone to expel the air. The Italians cook lungs with tomatoes and kidney beans, simmered for half an hour, the French cook lung stew (sometimes thickened with blood), and on Africa's Ivory Coast, the cud from cow's stomachs may be used as a sauce thickener.

Stomach—Once the stomach or tripe has been thoroughly cleaned it is usually cooked by simmering or stewing slowly in milk and chopped onion, and served in white sauce; or you can cut it into slices and fry with onion, vinegar, herbs and seasoning.

Sweetbreads—the testes, thymus and pancreas have the reputation of sharpening your mind and body. Sweetbreads are often considered a delicacy. Try them fried in batter or grilled with cheese. Testes are usually skinned then sliced and sautéed in butter.

Tails—Skin and disjoint the tail before cooking. Good for soups and stews.

Hooves and trotters—Soak in boiling water for a minute, which makes it possible for the horny outer foot to be pulled off, leaving 'cow-heels'. These are cooked firstly by simmering them in water or stock for about 3 hours (until the meat comes loose from the bones). Remove the bones, and continue cooking the meat either in a sauce, or by coating the meat in batter and frying it.

Using Your Head
Wash out the mouth; clean and wash the ears; and you could cut off the end of the nose to remove the sinuses. Furry heads, as of sheep and lion, may be de-furred by putting them briefly in the flames of a fire. All types of head may be cooked with the skin left on.

The simplest way to cook it is bake the complete head in hot ash under a fire. To eat, pick off the thin covering of meat, then open the brains.

A calf's head (or any head that fits in a big cookpot) is sometimes stewed whole, but first should be skinned and soaked in salted water for 12 hours (change the water twice) and rinsed in fresh water. Then put it in a pot of fresh water and heat it to boiling point. Skim off the scum, add vegetables, and simmer it all for about 2 hours. Thicken the liquid to make gravy.

Cheeks—ox-cheek is often cut off the face and cooked separately. Before cooking, soak it in salted water, as with a calf's head. Then boil it in a pot of water, skim the surface, add vegetables and simmer for about 3 hours. Make gravy from the liquid.

Pig's cheek is prepared the same way, but after simmering in water it is usually skinned and baked.

Ears—Pig's ears are eaten roasted, stuffed and baked, or boiled then cut in slices and fried. The cooking time should be about 2 hours. When I was given a pig's ear for breakfast one day in New Guinea it was baked in ashes and served with a crocodile egg. Bacon and egg—but it seemed a far cry from the traditional English breakfast.

Brains—Brains may simply be cooked in the animal's head, or treated in ways to make them more appetising. For good results, soak the brains in salted water for an hour or two, then detach and discard the skin and fibres. Put the brains in a pot with a chopped onion, a little vinegar or lemon juice, and lots of water. Simmer it all for 15 minutes. Then take out the brains and let them dry. Slice them thinly, coat them in seasoned flour or batter and fry them till browned.

Or simmer the slices in white sauce with a dash of lemon juice. Many French recipes add spinach purée. Indonesians cook brains in coconut cream. You can make brain-cakes by simmering the brains, then chopping them finely, seasoning and mixing with beaten egg to bind them. Heat the mixture until it thickens, then cool it. Divide it into cakes, coat them with egg and breadcrumbs and fry them until golden-brown.

Tongue—Soak the fresh tongue in brine overnight if you want the usual pink-coloured result, otherwise it will come out a greyish brown.

Put the tongue in a cookpot with plenty of cold water and some herbs. Bring it to the boil, skim off the scum, and simmer until the meat is tender (2 to 4 hours depending on size). Then put the tongue to cool. When it's cool enough to hold, peel off the skin, and cut away any inedible bony bits around the root. Place the tongue tightly curled in a pot, and leave a heavy weight on top of foil to press the tongue down. Leave until cold. Slice the tongue thinly for eating.

And here are a few helpful points on various animals.

Elephant

When this big game meat is killed, it becomes a special occasion for feasting in all the surrounding villages.

Among Europeans, the elephant's trunk is considered a delicacy. Treat it like tongue; cook it, then cool it before skinning. Slice thinly and enjoy hot or cold.

The early African explorer, Thomas Baines, also recommended eating the feet. This recipe was included in his diaries:

Dig a hole, make a fire in it until the sides and surrounds are well-heated, then rake out the fire. Cut off the front foot of the elephant at knee joint, place it in the hole, cover with embers and hot earth. Make a new fire on top, light it, and let it burn all night.

In the morning the meat is ready. Best eaten warm.

Kangaroo

In Australian road accidents between kangaroos and cars, often the car gets buckled, and the kangaroo lopes away unhurt. Kangaroo meat is dark and strong-tasting. The tail is the best part; cut it into steaks across each bone-join. It should be cooked with a rich brown sauce. Stewed kangaroo is recommended, and sometimes it is cooked in a curry.

Lion

Lion meat is red with a difference, since it belongs to the cat family. Bleed, skin and gut a lion in the same way as a bullock.

If slowly pot-roasted, lion meat can taste like baby beef.

Pork

Bleed and gut as for cattle, but don't skin a pig. Its bristles can be singed off in the fire when you cook the meat. Rub the skin with salt and fat before or during cooking to make crispy crackling. Very thick skin means that the pig is old, and if the meat looks clammy, it is not fresh.

A pig carcase is generally butchered into two half-carcases, and divided into different cuts from beef. The whole hind legs are good for roasting; the spare-ribs (perfect for barbecueing) come between the neck and the shoulderblade. The blade-bones also roast well. The front legs (called hands) are usually boiled in salted water. There is good meat all along its back; roast it. The thicker meat at the end of the back should be cut into large chops for frying or grilling. For stewing and soup, use the belly, knuckle, trotters and the head. Cheek is especially tasty.

Pork should be well cooked, and even if using a quick method like frying, the meat should remain cooking for at least half an hour. This is because pork is very susceptible to tapeworms, and they take a lot of cooking before they're dead.

Also when cooking pork, remember to keep basting it as the meat tends to get dry.

Bacon—Salted bacon slabs may be carried without refrigeration for about a week in warm climates (less if very hot) and can be kept longer if you first rub the bacon with vinegar. Slices of bacon need to be rubbed with plenty of salt and stored cold for a week before they're properly cured, but they should then be good for several weeks of travelling.

Wild Pig

An aggressive animal, but its meat is superb. Especially good when cooked slowly in a ground oven.

Pigs are a traditional unit of currency in the Highlands of Papua New Guinea, and the clans make extravagant displays of their wealth by holding 'Pig-kills'. It's not uncommon for three hundred pigs to be slain as a demonstration of a village's wealth. At a pig-kill I saw, the animals were tied to rows of posts. Neighbouring villagers had been invited and everyone milled around inspecting the pigs. The men wore large mushroom-shaped wigs of human hair decorated with red and yellow everlasting daisies, and feathers from birds of paradise. Their faces were painted with ochre, the predominant pattern being thick red lines round their eyes, and a red-coloured nose. It looked grotesque, but I suppose it was meant to.

Then, one by one the people clubbed the pigs to death. The bodies were butchered and distributed; much of the meat went into a *mumu* (ground oven), along with sweet potatoes, red pandanus fruit and juicy green leaves.

Rhino
The hump of the white rhino is eaten as a delicacy. Make a ground oven slightly larger and deeper than the hump. Cut a flap of rhino skin which is large enough to cover the open end of the hump, and skewer it over the hump as a lid. Put the hump in the hole; fill in the hole with embers and light another fire on top. Keep the fire burning all night; the meat will be ready in the morning. The thick-skinned hump makes a good dish and is full of rich juices.

Sheep and Goats
In Africa, goats and sheep tend to look alike, and both usually have tough meat. For best results it needs to be tenderised and cooked slowly. The liver and kidneys of young lamb (up to 3 months old) are among the most esteemed varieties, and their sweetbreads are also considered delicious. Castrated males taste better than billygoats. The haunches provide the best roasting meat. The head and neck of small kids are generally used for soup. It's undoubtedly nourishing.

Dried Meat
In the last century African explorers sometimes cured meat by putting thin strips of it under the horses' saddles.

As the men rode along, the horses' heat and sweat (salt) effectively cured the meat. And it made first-class biltong if dried!

Dried meat gets its various names from the pioneering races who popularised it—biltong from the Voertrekking Afrikaaners, or jerky from the American frontier. It is lightweight, nutritious and long-lasting; ideal for trekkers. It can be bought in some food shops, but it is easy to make from animals large or small.

Use lean red meat, or cut off excess fat (thick fat will go rancid). Cut the meat into long strips no more than 1 in (2½ cm) thick, running in the same direction as the meat fibre.

If the meat is very fresh you can squeeze out the blood by dipping it in water, then squeezing, re-dipping and squeezing until the meat is white. Meat dried without blood is less nutritious, but it will re-hydrate when cooked with liquid. Meat dried with blood cannot be re-hydrated, but tastes nicer for chewing.

Rub the strips of meat with salt and black pepper, and leave them for a day in extra salt. Alternatively, heat a solution of a tablespoon of salt to each cup of water until it starts steaming, then put the meat in it for a minute. (If you like, add a bit of garlic, or vinegar, or lemon, onion and herbs.) The meat should turn greyish.

Take it out, and grind black pepper over it—pepper is good for keeping the blow-flies off during outdoor drying.

Hang the strips of meat to dehydrate in a warm dry place. Sunshine and a dry wind are helpful outdoors; indoors an airing cupboard will suffice, but put a dish below the meat since it may drip. In four days the meat should be ready. The right dryness is when it can be slightly bent without splitting.

If packed away from direct sun and damp, biltong can stay good for years. It doesn't need cooking, just use a sharp knife to cut small slices, and chew them when you're hungry.

Cooked meats can be dried in the same way and will

store well for months. Cut off excess fat and if the meat was cooked in fat, wash this off in boiling water. Dried cooked meat can be re-hydrated by cooking it again in liquid.

Raw meat may also be preserved by soaking it overnight in the juice of lemons or limes mixed with salty water. Use 2 cups of fruit juice for each cup of salt water. Cut the meat into thin strips or slices. The citric acid effectively 'cures' the meat. I don't know how long it stays good, but probably for ages if you dry it after soaking.

Smoked meat—A traditional village method of preserving meat is by smoke-curing. The meat is put on a grid over a smoky smouldering fire. It takes a few days to cure it properly; the time depending on the quality of the smokiness and the size of meat. If you smoke the meat very dry it'll stay good for months; if it is not very dehydrated, it is good for a week or so. It won't re-hydrate unless you previously de-blooded it, but it doesn't need cooking before eating.

Remember that the flavour is affected by the type of woodsmoke. Oak gives a lovely flavour, as does apple, pear or cherry wood. In the tropics maize-cobs, acacia trees and thorn bushes provide good-flavoured smoke. It helps to dampen the wood to make the fire smokier, or sprinkle it with damp sawdust.

Vacuum-dried, heat-dried, and freeze-dried foods are available nowadays in shops. With such processes meat is dried in steaks, chops, chunks, hamburgers and meatballs. Vacuum- and freeze-dried meats take up more space than heat- or air-dried meat, but they re-hydrate faster in liquid.

11 Small Game and Poultry

The creatures in this chapter are slightly easier to tackle for the pot than those in Chapter 10. But remember, just because an animal is small does not mean its meat is tender, and you should still take the usual considerations of age and season of the year into account.

Rabbit and Hare
Kill with a sharp blow on the back of the neck and de-gut soon after death. Hang briefly to drain the blood. The carcase may be hung in cold airy shade for a few days until you need it, which makes the flesh more tender. Using a sharp knife, slit the rabbit's skin open from the chest across the belly and up between the hind legs to the tail. Take care not to cut into the entrails. When the belly-skin is open the entrails are easily removed; just tip them out.

To skin a rabbit, cut off the feet at the lower leg-joints, slit the skin from the back of each hind leg up to the tail, cut off the tail, ease the skin off the back legs and pull it up over the rabbit's rump. Hold its back legs firmly and peel the skin forwards to its neck; it should come smoothly.

Sever the neck and remove its head, and pull the whole skin downwards off its front legs. The belly-skin may simply be cut off. Wash the carcase inside and out.

If the meat smells very strongly, soak it in vinegar and water overnight. This draws out the blood and makes the meat whiter and much better-tasting. (If you're in a hurry, just soak it in salty water for an hour or two.) Rabbit meat is best when white; but hare meat should be red.

If you buy rabbit in the market, its flesh must look pink and fresh. Females taste better than males.

Dry the meat and chop it into joints before cooking it. Young ones may be roasted, but since they have little natural fat they do need to be basted. Old rabbits are best if marinaded and cooked as tough meat. Rabbit stew is particularly tasty if you add a cup of cider to the pot, or else a big spoonful of peanut butter. Simmer the stew for 2–3 hours.

Grey Squirrel

In autumn squirrels can be plump and good to eat. Old ones will improve if hung for a day (clean out the innards but leave the skin on and hang by the neck.) Skin and dress squirrel like rabbit. Tenderise the meat (see Chapter 12) before stewing, in a strongly-flavoured sauce. Young squirrels can be opened lengthwise in half and roasted over the fire.

Guinea-pig

Guinea-pigs are raised as meat in Peru, and provide fifty per cent of the national meat consumed.

Kill and prepare like a chicken. Don't skin it, just scald the fur and pluck it out. Gut the body and split it in halves lengthways. Soak the halves in salted water for 2 hours before cooking. Recommended grilled.

Monkey

This is the way I was taught to cook monkey. First make a fire and throw the carcase in the flames to singe off its fur. This is faintly gruesome as a dead monkey has the expression of a sleeping baby, but when the flames scorch its skin it shrivels, giving its face a sudden ugly snarl.

Remove the body from the fire and cut off its hands, feet, and head. Don't bother trying to skin the body, since monkeys are difficult to skin; and anyway the skin can be quite tasty. Wash it, remove its stomach, entrails and offal; keep the liver and kidneys; and cut the body into quarters or joints.

Fry the portions in fat or oil with pimentoes and

onions. When they are well browned add some water and leave it all to simmer for a couple of hours. The longer it simmers the better, for—as my teacher explained to me—monkey flesh has to be gnawed off the bone unless well-cooked; and he smiled, showing his teeth which were sharpened into points.

In flavour monkey-meat is between pork and mutton, but it can be rather strong. It is much improved if marinaded beforehand.

Opossum and Raccoon
Let it hang for a day in the cold if you are in no hurry. Clean and skin, removing the glands in the middle of its back and those in its front legs.

Divide the meat into big pieces. Boil them briefly, change the water and boil briefly again. Then dry and roast them, or cook in stew, or bake in damp leaves in a ground oven. They are traditionally eaten with sweet potatoes.

Porcupine and Hedgehog
To skin a porcupine, hang him by the hind legs spread wide apart, and cut open the skin on his belly (where there are no prickles). Ease the skin off in all directions with your hands. Actually it's not difficult. Then open the abdominal lining and remove the guts. Keep the liver, which is mild-tasting and good when fried.

The best meat is at the top and rear of the porcupine's back. The meat is dark and strong-looking, but it tastes like lamb-cum-pork. Young porcupine can be roasted, the old ones should be stewed or curried. Recipes from early colonials in West Africa recommend that the meat is served with plantain (cooking bananas).

Otherwise, to save trouble, you could just put a porcupine or hedgehog complete with quills into the fire. The quills will be burnt off. Then grill the meat over the embers.

Also, as mentioned earlier, if you roll a hedgehog (or porcupine) in a layer of wet clay, the clay will cake to its quills, and after cooking when you break the clay open, the quills are pulled out; leaving the meat ready for eating.

Frogs

Frog legs are a well known delicacy, though still, with the snails, which follow, an insular music hall joke. A frog can be caught if one person attracts its attention and another grabs it from behind! Remove the head, peel the skin off the body (often it contains glands with harmful secretions), and peel the legs. Roast the frog over a fire and when cooked, pick off the meaty bits. The back legs are best.

There are giant bullfrogs the size of chickens in many countries. The bushman of Botswana has an ingenious way of gutting them. He takes a deep breath, places his lips against the frog's anus and blows so hard that the frog's stomach and entrails are forced out through its mouth. Bushmen must have lungs as well developed as their buttocks. The body of the giant bullfrog has a fair amount of protein-rich meat which tastes slightly like chicken. The legs are best dusted in flour and fried with butter and garlic.

Salamanders are treated and eaten like frogs. Some of the big ones (over 20 inches or ½ a metre) may bite!

Snails

There are many different kinds of land snails, nearly all are edible, and they have provided high-protein food for man since Neolithic times. Still popular in Europe, the French consume over 7 million kilos of snails a year.

To make snails clean themselves inside, put them in a potful of salted water, cover it firmly, and leave them to soak for half a day. Put them in clean water to cook, and boil or steam them until they come out of their shells. Then fry, or cook them in a strongly-flavoured stew.

Giant African Snails can be 6 in (15 cm) long. This is a recipe from the Ivory Coast: Smash the shell with a rock, pull out the snail and gut it. Discard the windpipe and entrails but keep the stomach (a long pale sac). Clean the slime off the snail's skin by rubbing with lemon. Cut the snail into chunks and put it in a pot with root vegetables, hot peppers, some water, and the stomach's milky contents. Simmer the pot for about 2 hours.

River snails—experts go along streams picking up snails with their toes. To cook river snails, boil them until they lose their shells, then fry them in butter and garlic.

To Prepare Poultry

To kill a chicken (or any fowl) wring its neck with a sharp twisting-pulling action. When you feel its neckbones give, stop, or you may pull its head off. Pluck the bird while it is still warm. Pull out the biggest feathers first. If the bird starts flapping, that's just nerve-reaction. Don't lose yours, and keep on plucking.

When an unplucked bird is left to grow cold, its feathers will set firm and be difficult to pull out. Should this happen put the bird in boiling water for a minute before plucking. Afterwards, singe off any remaining fluff in the flames of a fire.

Cut and break off the legs at the knees. Cut and sever the head from the neck at the top. Slit open the skin down the back of its neck and peel the skin away from the neckbone. Cut off the neckbone where it meets the body, leaving a flap of neck-skin (helps in cooking).

Put your finger in the neck-hole, feel around and take out the crop (a hard muscular bag that is full of gritty particles for grinding food—a bird's equivalent of teeth). Then feel down to the chest cavity and move your finger round in a circle to free the innards from the chest.

Turn the bird upside-down and slit a big hole in the skin just in front of the anus. Widen the hole, but take care not to break the gall bladder (its juice will make the bird taste sour). Slide your hand into the hole, putting the back of your hand against the inside back of the bird, and finish loosening the guts. The idea is to draw the guts out together with attached organs. Cut round the anus and take it out with the rest. The liver, kidneys and heart are useful for making stock, or else finely chopped in stuffing or gravy. Wash the bird out before cooking.

Old birds, destined for the pot, can be skinned complete with feathers; it is less bother than plucking. Start from the thighs, and peel the skin off upwards. Pull the skin with one hand, and hold the flesh down with the other. Or leave the bird complete with feathers and skin, and just roll the bird in clay for baking.

Younger birds are ideal for roasting. Spit the bird whole on a stick, or suspend it on string; or cut it open lengthways and flatten it into halves, for frying or barbecueing. (Scorch the cut surface first to seal in the juices.) If there's little natural fat, baste the bird during cooking with oil, fat, or a more interesting baste (see Chapter 12).

Wild Birds
Wild birds that are officially rated as pests (such as pigeon) may be killed during any season, though on private land you need the landowner's permission to be there.

The season for game birds is the autumn (they're generally protected by law during their breeding season), and the shooting rights belong to the landowner.

Rooks—Use only the breast and leg meat since the rest tastes bitter. Skin the bird and soak the good meat overnight in salted water (makes it less bitter), or marinade it.

Traditionally in rural England, rooks are cooked in pies.

Water birds—Coot and moorhen inhabit fresh-water ponds. Pluck (or skin) and gut the birds before cooking in stew. Wild ducks are less fatty and more tasty than domestic ones. Ducks should be plucked and gutted before cooking. If there's a thick fatty layer under the skin, prick into it with a fork to let the fat run. A popular Chinese recipe is for duck rubbed with a mixture of soy sauce, honey and an egg-yolk, then roasted over a fire. It is delicious.

All birds are edible, but, like animals, they taste of what they eat, and those which live on fish do taste fishy. Seagulls taste unpleasantly fishy. To negate a fishy taste stew the birds in vinegar with a spoonful of mustard seeds. (You could dilute the vinegar with some water, depending on how strong you wanted it.) Or else stuff the birds with salted raw onion and/or raw potato (which absorb the fishiness), and cook as normal.

Game Birds
In temperate climates hanging game birds by their necks with guts and feathers intact for several days increases the flavour of pheasants, partridges and grouse and tenderises their flesh. But if you're hungry, you don't have to wait.

Don't hang water birds as they are oily and will go rancid. Wash the flesh in very salty water (perhaps also add vinegar); repeat washing and soaking in a change of water, then rinse well. Put a little bag of cold crushed charcoal inside the bird. This is not to cook it inside out; it simply makes the meat taste sweeter.

Woodcock, snipe and quail—do not need hanging or gutting, only plucking, before being cooked. Leaving the entrails in is considered to make the bird taste better. If skinned, it is best to fry the meat; otherwise roast it for about 15 minutes over a fire.

Pigeon, wood-pigeon, guinea-fowl, and general bush-fowl—Kill and hang them upside-down for a few minutes to let the blood run to the head. Pluck the feathers while you wait. Then decapitate the bird, and remove the entrails, etc.

Their meat tends to get dry in cooking. Fry or roast and baste the young ones; stew the oldies.

Small wild birds don't need plucking or the removal of entrails; just burn off their feathers as you cook them in a fire. Usually only the breast and thighs are worth eating.

Thoughts about Eggs

Chicken eggs—in developing countries, are often rotten. At a market in Nigeria I bought some eggs, or so I thought—but the woman snatched them back, dunked them in a bowl of water, and gabbled crossly at me. It transpired that she was scolding me for not testing to see if the eggs were good. When put in water, good eggs sink, and rotten ones float. Mine all floated. The woman laughed heartily and chose some others for me.

The eggs of wild birds whose nests are easily robbed do not usually taste pleasant. Birds that hide their nests lay the best-tasting eggs.

If you make a pin-prick hole in the top end of an egg, you can cook it upright on the fire's embers.

Ostrich eggs—are very rich and creamy. One ostrich egg is equal in content to 24 chicken eggs, or nearly two litres of egg. It is excellent scrambled. Or cook it in its shell (break open the top, and sit the egg on the embers until suitably cooked). However, beware of ostriches! The males are aggressive, and attack by striking with one leg, which has a fighting claw that can rip your belly open. If you can't escape attack, I'm told you should lie flat on the ground.

Iguana eggs—are a delicacy in Central and South America. They are usually fried or pickled.

Turtle eggs—the shell is very leathery. The egg tastes better roasted than boiled. (Don't bother with tortoise eggs. They taste like dust.)

Crocodile eggs—they're duck-egg-sized but oblong. They have a white yolk, and taste much like chicken eggs.

Dried eggs—People's reactions to the idea of dried eggs are a great age give away! Those who are allergic to the notion probably lived through a surfeit of them in the Second World War. But dried eggs are a really useful source of important protein for campers. Heat-dried and freeze-dried eggs have almost the same nutritional value as fresh eggs. You can use dried egg powder instead of fresh eggs in most recipes, and it works well for things like scrambled eggs or omelettes.

A dozen eggs in powder form weigh about 4 oz (115 g).

To make egg powder, take about a dozen eggs, and separate the whites from the yolks. Beat the yolks until smooth, and pour the liquid on to a tinfoil-lined tray, spreading the yolk thinly over it. Dry it slowly in a gentle oven heat. When almost dry, it helps to chop it up a bit, crumble it, and dry it again. When it is thoroughly dry and leathery, crush it to fine powder, and wrap it up.

Put the egg whites in a bowl and whisk them until stiff (as for meringues). Add a teaspoon of cream of tartar, and whisk again. Then spread this mixture thinly on tinfoil on a tray and dry it also in a slow oven. When it is completely dry, crumble it into powder, and wrap it separate from the yolks.

Dried eggs stay good for months if stored away from direct heat, damp and sunlight.

To re-make one egg, take a big spoonful of yolk powder and the same of white, and mix them with 2 or 3 spoons of water. Let the mixture stand for about 10 minutes until it thickens.

12 Meat Cookery

Experienced chefs can skip this chapter of basic advice to bush cooking amateurs, but if you do you'll miss my speciality peanut butter stew and salivary gland-jerking bastes.

A Good Stew

Stew is the staple diet of campers, so it's worth knowing how to make it taste good. Poorer cuts or any tough meats are usually all right for stewing. Divide the meat into lumps, cutting across the grain of fibre as much as possible. Birds and rabbits should be divided into joints.

There are two ways of cooking stew: either coat the meat thickly in flour and fry it, then add stock or water and simmer the whole stew for a couple of hours; or simmer the meat and vegetables in liquid, and just before the end of cooking remove a cupful of liquid to mix with a tablespoon of flour, then return it to the stewpot. The gravy will gradually thicken. Let it simmer to make sure the flour gets cooked for about thirty minutes before serving. The first method is usually tastier, but if the fire is too hot the thickened gravy may burn on the sides of the pot.

I prefer to take my chances and use the first method, frying the meat coated in flour with chopped onion until browned, then adding seasoning, vegetables of different colours, a few edible roots or some nuts and mushrooms; and topping up the stewpot with enough stock or water to cover everything.

Bring it to the boil then put a lid on the pot and leave it simmering on low heat for 2 to 3 hours. The tougher the meat, the longer it needs cooking. You could bury the stewpot in the warm remains of the fire and cover it with

116

earth (or put it in a haybox) to cook overnight or during the day while you're away from camp. If the gravy is not thick enough, thicken it again with flour and re-heat to simmer. If you have no flour, try using alternative thickeners such as dried soup, glutinous plants, sea-weeds (carrageen or laver), mashed potato, or any other mashed tubers or taproots.

Make plenty of stew; it is good to have too much as leftovers may be re-boiled and usually taste even better. When re-heating leftover stew, it must be boiled for 3 minutes to kill bacteria, then simmered briefly before serving.

Don't forget the dumplings—they should be added for the last 20–30 minutes of the stew's cooking. Make dumplings out of flour, fat, salt and water, mixed into a thick paste. (You could add milk powder, dried egg or baking powder; or use any of the dough recipes in Chapter 9.) Or just make dumplings from stale bread, dampened and squeezed until doughy.

Don't make the dumplings too big and heavy; they should rest partly submerged on top of the stew. Remove the lid from the pot for the last 15 minutes of cooking.

If stew is your staple diet, vary it occasionally. Try adding some legumes, turn it into chilli con carne; put a tablespoonful of tomato paste in the gravy; or stir in some freshly grated coconut. After long cooking it releases a deep mellow flavour. The same goes for peanuts. Nigeria is famed for its peanut stew, made by crushing and adding a handful of roasted peanuts to the stewpot. My speciality is to use a tablespoon of chunky peanut butter, which gives a deliciously creamy-nutty taste.

Gravy and Sauce

The dullest bits of food can be made tasty and interesting with gravy or sauce. When you fry meat or roast it in a container, you get excellent fat for making gravy. Leave the brown crunchy fragments from cooking in the fat, as they're good for flavour. Gravy is my speciality. I don't know why, but it always seems to taste superb.

Using roughly a tablespoon of melted fat, stir in an equal-sized quantity of flour, making a paste. Add some seasoning and let the paste fry for a moment. Just before it burns, pour stock or water slowly into the pan, stirring continually to rub out lumps as the mixture thickens and bubbles. Keep adding liquid little by little until the gravy reaches the required consistency. (If you pour the liquid in too fast the gravy will go lumpy.) Let it simmer for a minute to ensure it is cooked. When made with stock rather than water, gravy is much tastier.

Once you've mastered the making of gravy, you can use the same method for making virtually any kind of sauce. Here are three of my standbys.

Nut sauce—use butter, flour and stock for the base, and add coarsely-ground nuts, some raisins, cinnamon, and lemon-juice. (Good with chicken and white meats.)

Sweet and sour sauce—put 4 tablespoons of brown sugar, 4 tablespoons of vinegar, a pinch of salt and half a mug of chicken stock into a pan over a fire, and bring it to the boil. Then mix a tablespoon of cornflour with a tablespoon of soy sauce, and add it to the pot. Simmer for a couple of minutes, until it thickens.

Barbecue sauce—for a mild barbecue sauce use equal quantities of vinegar, water and tomato ketchup; a little sugar, a dash of mustard and/or Worcestershire sauce and seasoning. Mix it all together, bring to boil, and simmer for 5 minutes.

Bastes
Meat which has little fat (poultry, veal and lean animals) should be kept moist by occasional basting during cooking.

The simplest baste is melted fat. (If you're cooking in a pan, or if you've got a drip-pan to catch the meat's runaway juices, spoon the juice and fat back on top of the meat.)

Melted butter with lemon juice and chopped herbs is an easy alternative baste, while soy sauce mixed with water and some honey is terrific.

The consistency of a baste may be thin or thick. The thicker the baste the better it clings to the meat, but it should only be used during the last half of cooking time or it may get burnt.

Good combinations are:

- orange juice, marmalade, Worcestershire sauce, wine-vinegar, herbs and seasoning
- pineapple juice, tomato paste, soy sauce, oil, lemon powder, and brown sugar
- red wine, honey, soy sauce, and ginger
- honey and mustard, fruit juice, etc
- lemon juice, oil, wine or cider-vinegar, Worcestershire sauce, garlic, curry powder and seasoning

A guide to the right quantities is to use equal amounts of things like wine or vinegar, oil, and fruit juice; a quarter as much soy or Worcestershire sauce; and a large pinch of seasonings. Taste it to decide if it needs more sweetness.

Oven Roasting

Roasting needs fierce heat and tender meat. The most suitable things for oven roasting are whole birds, or joints of meat such as rib, loin, leg (of ham) and shoulder.

Pot Roasting or Braising

This is more like a steaming or baking process. It is suitable for small joints of tough meat and poorer cuts like brisket, chuck steak and topside.

Spit-roasting

Spit-roasting is convenient for whole birds or animals, provided their meat is tender. Firstly, gut and clean the carcase, pluck birds' feathers, and skin all animals except pigs, monkeys, and others with edible skin.

Peel and sharpen a suitable pole for a spit, and push it through the animal so the pole comes out at the base of the neck. The carcase has to be evenly balanced if the spit is to turn properly. Tie the legs close to the body, or they will burn.

A pig takes about eight hours to spit roast, an ox takes a full day. Small animals and big birds take about an hour.

Here's a method to get the spit to turn itself. Hang the chicken, or whatever, about 8 in (20 cm) from the fire's heat by a string attached to its hind legs and tied at the top to an overhanging tree or a cross-pole between uprights, at least 3 ft (1 m) high. The higher the better. The string—or you can use a thin pliant strip of bark—should be dampened before use, so that it will not burn through. If the string is long enough, the wind will make the bird rotate, slowly twisting and untwisting the string. You could give it a spin to start it off. If the breeze is not enough, slide a piece of something flat and straight (card or bark) through the top of the string to catch what breeze there is.

Another advantage of this method is that by putting a dish below the chicken you will catch the juices, and can use them to baste the skin during cooking.

When barbecueing portions of a bird over the fire, cook the flesh side first, quickly scorching it to seal in the juice. As with all meat, after initial scorching, move it a few inches further away to cook. Don't add salt since it draws out the juice.

Is It Done?

To test whether the meat is cooked, pierce it with a sharp point and judge from the colour of the juice that seeps out. If it is too bloody, cook it more, and when the colour looks appetising, it's ready. An ordinary-sized steak takes about 15 minutes, and a large slab of beef cooks in about 40 minutes. For white meat and poultry the juice will be clean and watery when the meat is ready for eating. A small chicken (opened in halves) cooks in about 30 minutes.

Tough Meat
Camping and tough meat seem to go together. This is because the less sought after cuts of meat tend to be tough, and because country-folk prefer to kill old or mature animals which are stringier than young ones; and if the countryside has poor grazing, the meat raised there is usually tough. Nice and chewy is one thing, but it's a shame when meat is near inedible.

In small villages a traveller sometimes receives the honour of being offered a chicken. Then comes the chase. A terrified squawking rooster flaps past hotly pursued by barking dogs and a horde of small children brandishing sticks and stones. Their shrieks of excitement recede into the distance as the rooster runs for his life. Maybe an hour later the chase will return, still in hot pursuit, until the chicken falls over exhausted. Its meat is not going to be tender.

Tenderising meat—the most obvious ways are by stewing or pot-roasting, since the longer and slower the cooking the more tender the meat becomes.

An instant way to make uncooked meat less tough is to hammer it with a stone or a wooden mallet. (Make a mallet from a back-forked branch.) Hammer the meat hard all over to break up its fibres. Then grill, fry, or stew it.

Pawpaw (papaya) provides a marvellous tenderiser. Cook the meat (or poultry) wrapped in pawpaw leaves or in the fruit-skin, in a ground oven; or put an unripe fruit into your stewpot; or if you wish to roast or barbecue the meat, you should soak it overnight in fresh pawpaw juice. I believe there is nothing that the juice can't tenderise. The Chinese say you can get a good result simply by hanging old poultry from the pawpaw tree itself. Powdered pawpaw tenderiser is available nowadays in some modern supermarkets.

Alternatively, you could soak meat for a while in a marinade to tenderise it, and make it extra delicious.

Marinades

Marinades are made from a combination of tenderising acid, oil for juicing up lean meat, and seasoning to bring out the meat's flavour. The tenderising acid may be vinegar, wine or juice of citrus fruit, or things like cider, beer or yoghourt. The oil could be any food oil or fat such as butter, margarine, lard, or dripping. The seasoning is salt, pepper (ideally black) and herbs or spices, and maybe chopped onion.

A basic formula is:

1 cup of leftover red or white wine (or a tablespoonful of vinegar)	some salt and a few peppercorns a big pinch of herbs
2 tablespoons of vegetable oil	

Put the mixture in a bowl or pot with the meat, and leave it to soak.

Cookery books often tell you to use enough marinade to cover the meat, but in my opinion this is unnecessary; it is just as effective to use a little marinade and turn the meat over occasionally.

For a large hunk of meat, soak it for 8 hours (overnight); smaller pieces of meat need only a few hours; and bite-sized lumps are vastly improved after an hour.

If the meat is strong, choose a marinade that will give it flavour; if the taste is delicate you need simply to enhance it, or give it spice. Red meat goes with dark vinegar or red wine, and white meat with pale vinegar, cider, white wine, lemon juice, and so on.

Use your imagination to adapt marinade recipes, and improvise with whatever you can find. With beef I'd suggest something like:

1 mugful of red wine or sherry (or a tablespoonful of vinegar)	sliced orange peel 4 big spoons of brown sugar few drops of Worcestershire sauce
2 tablespoons of vegetable oil	salt, pepper and mixed herbs

An interestingly spicy option is:

1 mugful of tomato juice	1 chopped onion
3 spoonfuls of vinegar	1 clove of garlic
1 spoon of olive oil	a sprinkling of ginger
½ spoon of sugar	allspice
a liberal dash of Worcestershire sauce	salt

Or how about peach juice or pineapple juice mixed with a cup of yoghourt, and some onion, garlic, salt, ginger and chilli powder. Or use cider or a can of beer mixed with a dollop of marmalade, 4 tablespoons of soy sauce, a tablespoon of brown sugar, a tablespoon of dry mustard, and a sprinkling of salt and ginger.

Veal and lamb marinades are good when made of equal parts oil and lemon juice, mixed with herbs and salt. For pork, try:

1 mug pineapple juice	1 tablespoon brown sugar
½ mug wine-vinegar	1 teaspoon dry mustard
1 tablespoon tomato paste	1 teaspoon chilli powder
1 tablespoon Worcestershire sauce	salt and pepper

This is delicious and can be used as a marinade, baste or gravy. It is especially good with pork spare-ribs for a barbecue.

If you think that poor-quality meat only deserves poor cookery, read the following menu. It was for a dinner which took place in Paris, during the Siege of Paris in 1870. I think the meal was held at the Ritz after they'd been killing off the animals in the Paris Zoo. My translations are put in brackets.

Le Grand Dîner Parisien

MENU

Potage: Purée Crôuton-Imperiale (bread soup)

Hors d'oeuvres: Sardines Anté-Diluviennes (very very old sardines)

Consommé de Tire-Fiacre (cab-horse soup)

Entrées: Galantine de Mufles (cow's snouts)

Andouillettes Boudins de Dada (horse-meat sausages)

Rat à la Crapaudine (rat-in-the-hole! with batter)

Haricot de Chien (dog stew)

Cheval à la mode (dish of horse-meat)

Civet de Lapin de Gouttières (gutter-rabbit, probably cat)

Rôtis: Gigot d'Antelope (haunch of antelope)

Mulet, âne, cheval (mule, donkey, horse)

Filet d'Éléphant (elephant-steak)

Patrons were asked to bring their own bread.

13   *Unusual Eatables*

It is not that all the creatures listed in Chapters 10 and 11 are what you would expect to find in a supermarket freezer cabinet. But here we get into the real exotica—from our point of view. Elsewhere they are familiar food. So have the courage to push back a few gastronomic frontiers. Don't waver. Take strength from a bit of role reversal fantasy and imagine a Sepik tribesman from Papua New Guinea facing up to a fish finger.

Turtles

Turtles and terrapins can be caught on a baited hook or in a fish-net. They are sometimes available in coastal fish markets, or in tropical village markets near big rivers. Live ones may be displayed for sale in bunches of five, joined by strings through a hole in their shells, every turtle facing outwards, so that although they all scrabble hard to get away, each one's efforts merely counteract the others'. It is a pathetically comical sight.

The simplest way to prepare and cook a turtle is to bury it in the fire's embers (or a ground oven) for an hour, then eat it from its shell. The best meat is in the legs, and lining the shell; the meat is white, with the taste and texture of shellfish.

Some species of turtle, such as 'Stick Pot', have odoriferous glands; when you cook them they smell terrible. Boil them and change the water twice to get rid of the smell. Then cook as normal.

Tortoise

This can be cooked by roasting it in its shell upside-down in the fire. When cooked, remove it from the fire and chop off the sides of the tortoiseshell. Dig out the flesh.

Most of the interior is occupied with stomach, but there is a thick meat lining along the shell. The legs also contain good meat; peel them before eating. The meat can be stewed with spices, or grilled on kebabs. It tastes not unlike chicken.

Armadillo
Cleaned and stuffed with chopped vegetables, armadillo can be baked in its shell. It needs some basting or the meat gets dry.

Crocodile
Crocodile tail is a delicacy, a white fish meat which tastes similar to lobster. In fact I've heard of a factory in Zimbabwe producing canned crocodile under the label 'Mock Crayfish'.

To catch a crocodile is not easy. They are both armour-plated and surprisingly agile. I was once chased by a crocodile on dry land, and it moved alarmingly fast. Crocodiles are only really vulnerable in one patch at the back of their forehead behind the skull bone.

Ideally, crocodiles for eating shouldn't be longer than 6 ft (2 m). If larger, the flesh smells strong and musky.

When I met up with local crocodile hunters in the Sepik we hunted the creatures by night. While one man paddled the dugout canoe smoothly across the lake, the other man began slapping the water with his hands, then cupping his hands over his mouth to call, '*Nuark-nuark.*' On one occasion I heard a crocodile reply, with the same *nuark-nuark* sound.

The men used a strong flashlight to spot the crocodiles, which often floated on the water's surface, watching us. When I flashed my torchbeam around the lake I could see innumerable glittering eyes, like galaxies of red stars. When a suitable crocodile came within range the hunter hurled a carved spear attached to a long bush-fibre rope. There was instant commotion; the creature thrashed and flailed in the water, then it bolted. The hunter let it go quite far before he pulled the line taut, then started playing it, as a fisherman plays a fish. After exhausting the crocodile he brought it alongside the canoe, and the second man was ready for it with a machete.

Their hunting tactics during daytime are definitely not recommended for amateurs: they just walk around in the lake, chest-deep in water, feeling for crocodiles with their feet.

The folklore of the Sepik people is interwoven with crocodiles. During the three months I paddled a canoe round the Sepik river and its tributaries I was fortunate to see one of the tribal rituals associated with the crocodile. The festivities took a week and they climaxed with the skin-cutting ordeal, when the initiates' chests and backs were cut open in dramatic patterns to represent crocodile scales. Right at the end of the ceremony they cut the crocodile mark on my arm giving me the highest honour they could bestow. It is a scar I bear with pride.

To skin a crocodile—turn the body upside-down and, with a very sharp knife, slit open the belly skin from front legs to back legs (don't puncture the belly-lining). Then slit the front and back legs down their pale inner sides. Peel the skin away from the belly-lining, and use your knife to flay the skin off the rest of the body. If you want a good skin for posterity, it is slow and meticulous work. The skin-traders could do it in 15 minutes, but it took me over an hour.

After skinning, clean the crocodile. Cut open the belly-lining and tip out the entrails. But be particularly careful not to break the digestive organs; the stomach enzymes are fiercely poisonous.

To cook a crocodile—The best meat is in the tail. Cut steaks of it to roast over the fire. Pick the rest of the meat off the body to roast on skewers, or dice it and fry it with butter and herbs. Also good in soups and stews.

Lizard and Iguana
You will be more successful if you try catching them in the early morning, when they're sunbathing but still sleepy.

Grill them over the fire's embers. They have very little meat and aren't worth the bother of preparation. Just pick out the meat (the best is in the tail) when cooked.

In Mexico I tried stewed iguana meat (far tastier than lizard), and in Papua New Guinea there was dragon meat from the Salvadori dragon, which grows up to 12 ft (4 m) long. It is a type of monitor lizard and is actually quite timid.

Snake
Cut off the head and at least a further 3 in (7½ cm) from the body, since the poison glands are usually situated just behind the head.

If it is a poisonous snake, check it hasn't bitten itself; and should you find the tell-tale fang marks, don't eat the snake. Skin the snake by slitting along its underside, and peel off the skin. Peel the guts out, wash the snake, then wrap it in damp leaves and cook it in a ground oven.

To cook snake in its skin—let the fire die low, spread the hot embers, and coil the snake over the embers until its scaly skin is lightly scorched. Then, holding its tail in one hand, pull its body through your other hand so the scales are brushed off. Re-coil the snake on the embers and leave it until cooked. Open it and remove the entrails before eating, or just pick round them.

In the USA they have annual rattlesnake-roundups which are wild and drunken cowboy occasions. You can also buy tinned rattlesnake in some shops there.

Winged Mammals and Bats
Small winged mammals can be treated like squirrels. Vampire bats which live by blood-sucking are occasionally eaten by locals in South America, but are not recommended. Fruit bats or flying foxes, which live on bananas and tropical fruits, can be large and good to eat. Baked bat (a Samoan dish) is made by singeing the

fur off the bats, or skinning them, then cleaning and quartering the bodies before baking them in a ground oven.

Rats and Mice
Bush rats, cane rats, rice rats, wood rats, all types of rats which live on clean vegetable matter provide good meat. In the African bush, rats can grow as large as rabbits. They have little in common with town rats, which are scavengers.

The easiest way to prepare a rat is to put it on the fire whole, turning it to singe off the fur and whiskers. The singed fur can be scraped off with a knife. Gut and wash the body. Cut off and discard the feet and tail. Cut the rat into chunks and soak in water for an hour before cooking. The head is sometimes cooked whole, or crushed with stones to release juices that thicken the soup. Add salt and seasoning.

Alcoholic rats living in French wine cellars are grilled and esteemed for their flavour.

Mice-Field mice of many species are eaten in different countries. A simple Mexican recipe is to skin and clean the mice then skewer them as kebabs; an Arctic explorer recommends sautéed mice served in creamy sauce.

Grubs and Insects
Grubs and insects which feed on pure vegetable matter are wholesome and nourishing to eat. It is curious that we relish shrimps and crab, scavengers of the seabed, yet are repelled by the bugs of the land. Large grubs (*Prionus corioranus*) were kept and fattened for the table by the Ancient Romans, as a treat. Today the caterpillars of Skipper butterflies are canned for sale in Mexico, and many species are gathered by African villagers who eat them boiled, baked, smoked, or sun-dried. The freshly baked Hottentot speciality is sweet tasting and creamy. Red ant chutney is made in India by scalding the ants and grinding them to a paste with chillies and salt. While

in Zanzibar white ant pie is made by grinding together sugar, dried banana and white ants into a sort of honey-nougat paste.

Mopane grubs—The most commonly-eaten grubs are tree maggots, found under the bark of dead trees such as Mopane trees, sago palms and many other palms. Mopane grubs taste rather like shrimps. Boil the grubs in salted water, then fry or bake them. To eat, pull off their heads and squeeze out their innards.

Sago palm grubs are much larger (up to finger-sized). They're usually just boiled in water or roasted on the fire. The first time I ate sago grubs I didn't like them, but in the end I got used to them. What else can you do when someone brings you a bowl of grubs and says she spent the day in the forest finding them for you? However, I diplomatically managed to share them with her husband and children.

Woodlouse—The common European woodlouse (found under the bark of rotten trees) is said to taste like shrimp. One recipe suggests: kill the woodlice by dropping them in a cup of boiling water. Mix a little milk and butter with a teaspoon of flour and some seasoning in a small pan of water on the fire. When the mixture thickens, add the woodlice. The sauce goes well with fish.

Locusts and grasshoppers—Locusts contain almost three times as much protein as steak, and are eaten in many parts of the world. Remove their legs and wings, then pull off the head, drawing out anything that's attached. If you fry the bodies they taste oily, so try sprinkling them with vinegar or cooking them in curry. Grasshoppers can be fried in oil until crisp or roasted on the fire and eaten like roasted nuts. They mix well with peanuts.

Flying ants—Many white settlers in what was Rhodesia used to eat flying ants as a delicacy.

To catch flying ants you need a white sheet, a bowl of

water and a bright lamp. After dark put the light outside with the white sheet hanging in front of it, and the bowl of water at the foot of the sheet on the opposite side to the light.

Flying ants will be attracted to the light and, fluttering against the sheet, will slowly drop into the water. Not only do they drown, but also their wings fall off leaving them conveniently prepared for cooking. Strain the bodies out and put them in a pan over a fire. They contain enough fat to fry themselves. The result tastes rather like mushrooms fried in butter.

Very early one morning in Papua New Guinea as I floated slowly down the Sepik river in my canoe, I noticed several swarms of flying insects hovering just above the river. Gradually the air grew more dense with the insects, until I found myself inside a swarm that had no visible end.

The insects looked like grey earwigs with wings. They weren't interested in me, thank goodness, but just fluttered around busily between waterlevel and a few feet above it. It was curious how they kept diving at the water and skimming along its surface, and fluttering upwards to begin again. After about ten minutes of this there was still no end to the swarm, but something was happening. The grey flies seemed to be drowning, and other flying insects were starting to appear in their midst; I realised that I was watching the process of metamorphosis.

By skimming the river-surface the grey flies were making their skins split open, and when split, they fluttered frantically to free themselves of their old grey skins and wings. Discarded bodies littered the water as the new forms emerged, transformed into soft-looking pale-gold flying insects with long forked swallowtails trailing behind them.

I watched entranced while the air thickened with these dainty newcomers. River visibility was nil, my canoe-prow was a faint and blurred outline in a pale-yellow cloud. Occasionally I heard the splashes of fish jumping up to catch some insects, and birds came swooping down to grab them too.

That evening I stayed in a village, and for supper I was given a bowlful of the insects boiled for supper—it's odd how life turns out.

14   *Fish and Shellfish*

Before I began travelling I'd been a fussy eater, not
eating fish because I disliked the bones. But when I
found myself paddling a canoe down the Congo river
with my companion Lesley, our provisions were simply
some coffee, salt, bread and a jar of jam—we had decided
to live on fish.

On the first day of our voyage when a local fisherman
gave us a fish, I had difficulty keeping a smile on my
face while the fish writhed slimily in my grasp. I put it
down by my feet and we paddled on. About ten minutes
later the fish leapt flapping on to my legs; I screamed
and jumped, the dugout skewed sideways, hit a half-
submerged tree, and Lesley fell out into the river. The
canoe straightened up and sailed on, with me unable to
make it stop; I grabbed a branch of an overhanging tree,
which was full of red ants that ran down my arms and bit
me furiously. Then Lesley swam alongside and hauled
herself aboard, so I was able to let go. At noon we
stopped on an island in mid-river to cook our fish. Its
taste was worth all the trouble it had given.

Gradually as weeks passed we mastered the art of
canoeing, but we were seldom successful in catching
fish. We used hooks and lines, attached to our toes as we
paddled lazily downriver, but our biggest catch was a
fish that just jumped out of the water and into our canoe.

However, in six years of travelling since that time, I've
learnt many useful things about fishing.

The best times for catching fish are at dawn and dusk;
or after a rainstorm, and when an overcast sky begins to
clear. Also at night by torchlight—fish are attracted to
the light, rise up and can be caught with net or spear.
Beware, however, this is considered less than sporting
back home.

The simplest method for the fishing novice is hook and line. You don't need a rod. Just attach the line to a wooden block and run it through your fingers or toes, so you feel when there's a nibble. Bait is a topic of inexhaustible interest to serious anglers, but you can just experiment with what's about, like grasshoppers or caterpillars, woodbugs, wasps, or entrails of game. If you find yourself starting to take the business seriously you can always examine the stomach contents to see what the fish you've caught likes eating.

Spear fishing is a stylish looking activity, but calls for more skill or luck, or an alternative supper supply. Jab the spear into mud pools for fish like barbel, carp or pike, which bury themselves in muddy shallows. In clear pools remember to allow for refraction. You can make your spear from a strong straight hardwood stick with the point hardened in the fire. Bamboo is excellent and you can cut notches for barbs.

I've sometimes used my mosquito net for fishing, either as a fish trap in shallow water (funnel shaped – easy to enter, hard to leave), or simply to help scoop up tiny shoals which can be fried like whitebait.

Here's the classic method for tickling trout, given me by a gipsy. Look for them in cold fast-flowing streams and where the water widens into a pool with an overhanging bank. When you spot your trout move gently so it gets used to you. If it hides, wait. It will come out eventually. When you're ready, put your hand in the water behind the trout, move it slowly past its tail, and tickle the front half of its underbelly. Keep tickling for a minute, then take firm hold and pull the fish out of the water. Wearing Polaroid sunglasses helps you spot a fish, as long as you don't let them drop off with a splash in the excitement.

To Clean a Fish
The entrails should be removed fairly soon after catching. Cut a long slit in the underbelly, and run your finger inside to push out the innards. They usually

drop out as a neat unit. Keep any roe. Wash inside the fish.

The stomach in flat fish is just behind its head; cut round the head in a curve and pull the head away with entrails attached.

Scaling is easiest done using the back of your knife. Hold the fish tail and scrape the scales towards the head.

When buying fish in a market, check the eyes are bright, the gills are red, and the flesh feels firm. If you press the skin lightly with your finger, the mark should fade quickly if the fish is fresh.

Mud Fish

Mud wallowing fish like pike, carp, tench, and barbel which live on the lake bottom, can be muddy flavoured but will taste good if you keep them alive overnight in a bucket of clean water. Change the water twice, as the mud flushes out of the fish. Alternatively, follow this procedure: Cut off their heads and gills (including any gall-sac in the neck) and skin both sides of the fish. To do this, slice the skin from head to tail along the back, and on either side of the back-fin, then pull the back-fin out. Slit the belly-skin lengthwise, and make a circular cut round the fish's head and tail. Grip a corner flap of skin near the tail, and begin pulling the skin forwards. The skin must be wet, so hold it with a cloth or dip your fingers in salt. As you pull forward with one hand, use your other hand to hold down the flesh (and stop it from tearing up).

Next soak the mud fish for 2 to 3 hours in water and vinegar (in a ratio of 15 parts to 1), or salted water. This reduces the muddy taste, but the fish still needs cooking with herbs or something to give it flavour. Alternatively, simmer the fish for 20 minutes in plenty of salted water with herbs, then drain away the water since it will have absorbed mud. I suggest you make a separate sauce to eat with the fish.

Sauces can be buttery and seasoned; lemon-flavoured; white sauce with chopped parsley, or sorrel purée; rose-hip sauce, or tomato purée. In the tropics if you see a baobab tree with fruit, try the pale mushy fruit pulp with fish.

Eels and Elvers

To catch eels and elvers make a dangling bait of worms and wool, attached to a strong fishing line or string. Drop it in the river, maybe leaving it overnight. The eels get their teeth caught in the woolly bait and can be lifted by the line on to the bank. It can be very difficult to handle an eel, as it proverbially wriggles like mad. Hold it down with a cloth or newspaper and cut off its head.

To skin an eel, peel the entire skin backwards from the neck. If it is too slippery to grip, dip your fingers in salt. Don't pull the skin completely off if you want to cook stuffed eel. Gut it (the guts lie along its front half) and wash it, then coat the flesh with stuffing and pull the skin back over the top.

When stewing eels, peel the skin off completely, gut the body and stew it in sauce, or else cut it in bits and toss these in flour then fry until golden. Smoked eel is also popular and tasty: don't skin the eel, just gut it and coat it in salt overnight. Next morning, dip the eel in boiling water and hang it in smoke for several hours.

To cook elvers, fry them whole, or else drop them in boiling water for a minute, then dry and fry them; or chop them up with scrambled egg and tomato.

The conger eel is a sea creature. Cut it into steaks for grilling, or bake the whole thing slowly in seaweed in the fire.

Electric eels live in sluggish fresh-water rivers and lakes, and although eel-shaped they are in fact a South American fish related to carp. Their tails are capable of giving a shock up to 650 volts, usually only enough to stun not kill a man.

General Ideas for Cooking Fish

In all methods of cooking fish you should use maximum heat at first to sear the surfaces and hold in the flavoursome juices, then reduce the heat.

Medium-sized fish may be simply roasted on a stick (going through its mouth to tail) balanced above the fire's hot embers and basted with butter.

Barbecue wire isn't ideal when roasting fish, since the fish skin and flesh tend to fall apart during cooking. It is safer to put the fish on greased tinfoil, or wrap it in greased foil, or in damp leaves or seaweed, and bake it in the fire's embers. In the parcel with the fish I like putting mushrooms, chopped onion and any herbs (a sprig of fennel is good). Equally the fish may be stuffed with these things—anything herby, celery, lemon, mixed with leftover rice or breadcrumbs. In order to prevent the food drying out during cooking, add some butter, oil, fat, or liquid and close the foil by crimping the joins. Don't squeeze the parcel, but allow room for hot air. Bake in embers for about 15 minutes.

Fish should not be fiercely boiled, or cooked in a pot full of water—it takes away the flavour. Use only enough liquid to cover the fish, or less, but turn the fish occasionally. Simmer for 10 minutes per lb (450 g) of fish.

Tiny fish, such as small minnows and whitebait, are best fried whole in very hot fat, until they're crisp. Sprinkle them with salt and lemon.

Very big fish are best cut into steaks, and are nice eaten cold with mayonnaise. Don't try to store a big fish without ice, as it will certainly go off.

Smoke Cooking Fish

Suspend the fish by a stick through its gills, and prop its cleaned belly open with a short twig.

To make smoke-cured or dried fish for travelling, use the methods described for meat in Chapter 12.

Crustaceans

Crab—Salt-water crab are found in tidal rock pools or among seaweed and stones around the low tide mark. Cook crab by dropping it in a big cookpot with some seawater at the bottom, and cover the pot with a firm lid, or the crab will climb out. Heat the water to boiling point, then simmer for about 20 minutes. The crab will cook in the steam, and its shell goes red-brown when it's ready.

To open the body, put your thumbs under the tail-flap, push it upwards, and lift it off. Then turn the crab and push down on its mouth; the mouth and stomach should fall off. Discard the stomach sac, and the feathery 'dead men's fingers', located at the sides. The best meat is at the inner top of the back, and in the claws. Break open the legs and claws (claws open easily if you cut the ligaments).

Mix the crabmeat with seasoning, breadcrumbs, lemon juice, and French dressing, or with mayonnaise and parsley.

Lobster—They hide in crannies, but may be caught by diving for them or by dangling smelly meat bait around the seabed. When you catch something, pull the line in slowly, and be ready with a net since your catch will probably let go of the bait as it surfaces.

To clean lobster, punch a knifeblade through the brain from the top, and cut open the head, back and tail. Divide it into two halves. Remove the stomach which is just behind its mouth, and with a knife pick out its intestinal tube (a dark thin line going through the tail). The liver is edible, as is the coral, or roe, of the female.

When buying lobster in a fish market, make sure it is fresh by straightening the tail; if it doesn't curl back, it is not fresh.

Season the two halves with salt and black pepper, add a dab of butter and lemon juice, and grill the meat in its shells over a fire for about 15 minutes. Turn the shells upside-down for a few minutes at the end. When cooked, lobster shell is the familiar red. Never overcook shellfish.

If you have a cookpot large enough to hold a lobster (and with a tight-fitting lid), it may be easier to boil it in salted water. Bring to the boil, then simmer for 20–45 minutes, depending on size.

Crayfish—are smaller than lobsters. They are found in freshwater rivers, usually in limestone or chalky country. Crayfish can be caught by grabbing them from under rocks, or using a bait of smelly meat.

Crayfish may be cleaned and cooked like lobster, but they need less cooking time, only 5–10 minutes in boiling salted water.

Shrimps and prawns—both live in fresh or salt water. Salt-water shrimps are found at low tide in tidal pools, or by sandy river estuaries. Catch them in a net pushed under water along the sand, and cook them in a little boiling salted water for about 5 minutes. As soon as their shells turn pink they are cooked.

Thinking about shellfish makes me remember some months I spent horse-riding along the coast of the Transkei in Southern Africa. It was very wild with no coast roads and few people. Shellfish were abundant; sometimes I bought them from local fishermen, and sometimes I gathered them for myself. This kept me occupied while I waited beside river estuaries for the tide to turn, and the period of slack water when it would be safe enough to swim with my horse across each river, towing my saddlebags in the floating plastic sack behind us.

Sometimes I ate shellfish for breakfast, lunch and supper. The horse (who thought he could eat whatever I ate) once stole a mouthful of prawns, chewed them and spat them out. His expression was one I'll never forget!

Molluscs

Mussels, oysters, scallops and clams are the best. But beware of collecting them in polluted areas, such as near sewage outlets. The traditional European rule about only eating molluscs when there is an 'R' in the month should be observed, partly because the months without R include the breeding season, but mainly because the warmer summer temperatures increase bacterial growth in the water, which can turn the molluscs poisonous.

How to tell the good from the bad—discard first of all any whose shells are open or not tightly closed. Then proceed to the second check. Leave them in the sun for a few minutes, or over gentle heat, which makes their shells open, and discard any that stay closed. You can also tap the newly opened shells and they should snap shut. If they don't close, chuck them away. When you've sorted out the good ones, scrub the shells, and leave them overnight in clean salt water to flush out their systems. This routine is well worth observing for all the following molluscs. Eating dead or dying shellfish can make you very ill.

Mussels—Mussels are plentiful by the sea, attached to rocks and stones around the low tide mark. They also live inland, in fresh-water ponds.

The easiest way to cook most molluscs is to put a layer of damp seaweed on a fire, place the molluscs on the seaweed, and cover them with another layer of weed to keep the steam in. Otherwise, they could be cooked in boiling water for 5 minutes; simmered in cider; or simmered in white sauce with a little sorrel purée.

If not wanted for immediate eating, mussels will keep for several days in cold salted water.

Oysters—Nowadays oysters are difficult to find, but on wild rocky coasts at very low tide you may spot their knobbly shells in clumps growing off rocks. Prise open the oysters and eat them raw (swallow, don't chew). Or cook them lightly; they may be baked with seasoning, and a little butter and lemon.

Scallops—These decorative fan-shaped shells (the symbol of pilgrimage) are found in muddy sand at extra low tide (ie. new or full moon). Remove the innards, throw away the dark-coloured parts and keep the pale parts. Wash these well in salt water, and wash the shells also. Then replace the meat in the shells and cook them for about 3 minutes over a fire. Add a dab of butter. Or else poach or fry them with seasoning and lemon juice, breadcrumbs, butter, shredded onion and watercress.

Clams—Dig or rake them from the sandy mud above the low tide mark. Clams can be eaten raw, like oysters, though the simplest way to make them open is by steaming them for 5 minutes. They can be cooked like scallops, or in a creamy soup, and taste richly delicious.

Cockles—These are found by raking the muddy sand above the low tide mark. Where you find one you will probably find many more. Boil in sea water for 10 minutes. Eat with vinaigrette and salad; or else make soup of them with a little onion, garlic and parsley.

Conches and whelks—Hard-shelled sea-snails, often found in rocky inlets. Remove their 'door-stop'. Cook in seaweed on the fire, or in boiling water for 10 minutes. They're good in fritters.

Periwinkles and winkles—Their small long-pointed shells are found between tide levels. Make sure you put a lid on the pot they soak in overnight or they'll escape! Cook them in seaweed or boiling salted water for 10 minutes. You need a pin to eat them—to winkle them out of their shells. But they don't taste very good.

Razor-fish or razor-shells—Delicious baked or in soup if you can find them at extra low tides, but very difficult to catch since they burrow deep and quickly.

Limpets—I'm told you can get them off the rock by kicking them before they're aware of you. I think it's safer to use a knife blade.

To cook, bring to the boil in salted water, and simmer for 10 minutes, until the meat comes loose from the shells. Then fry or stew them till tender.

15 Edible Plants

In recent years enthusiasts like Richard Mabey have done a lot to educate us toward the possibilities of gathering a wide range of wild plants for food, and not just as make-do substitutes either. Comfrey, for instance, contains a higher protein level than any other vegetable except soya beans, while Fat Hen has more iron and protein than cultivated spinach.

I've only included the edible plants that are worth the trouble of gathering and are genuinely delicious. There are an awful lot more which are too spindly and indifferent tasting to be worth the effort.

Identification
A well illustrated handbook is the obvious method of finding your way round edible plants, and for temperate climates there are plenty on the market. But in remote parts the thing to do is pick a sprig of leaves or a plant top and ask local advice. Look, too, at what is on sale in local markets. Watch what other people are buying. (And what they pay, as well, then offer the same. It often saves you getting ripped off.) Don't think that if birds and animals eat something, it is safe for you, too. Very often it is, but not invariably. If you are in doubt try a very small amount of the plant, like a teaspoonful, and wait six hours to see if there are any ill effects. Don't indulge in a hearty meal of it until you've tested it at least twice. Bear in mind that a plant family may contain edible and poisonous relations. If you're not sure, don't eat it.

Where to Avoid
Don't gather plants from busy road verges where exhaust fumes will have spoilt their taste; nor in fields where

insecticides, weed-killers or fertilisers may have been used. And bear in mind chemical sprays can blow into adjacent fields. Don't pick plants growing in polluted water, since plants are largely made up of the water they absorb. This rules out water draining from sprayed or fertilised fields, water downstream of towns or villages, and tidal marshes near sewage outlets

Salad Themes

Raw plants are more nutritious than cooked ones. Most edible plants that are green in winter, such as cress, are suitable for salads. Remember wild plants have tough skins and are sometimes stringier than cultivated varieties, so pick them young and tender, up until flowering time, and wash well.

The trick of making salads that aren't boring is to blend different flavours, sweet and sour, bitter and bitter-sweet, spicy-hot and juicy-cool. Use more of the milder flavours, less of the sharp. Texture and colour can also play their part. If the basis of your salad is greenery, try using the young leaves and new shoots of brooklime, chickweed, burdock, daisy, dandelion or garlic mustard. You can vary the texture with crunchy roots of yellow goatsbeard or hawkbit. For colour sprinkle on the petals of red dead-nettle, marigold or dandelion.

Spinach-type Greens

These don't require extra water for cooking. Just put them wet from washing into the pot with some salt. Use plenty of leaves since they cook down to surprisingly little. Cover the pot and cook for 5 to 10 minutes. Then chop up the leaves and add a dollop of butter. You may find some forms of spinach are too bitter; if so, tear out the main leaf-rib before cooking, or add a little sugar during the cooking, or else add creamy things such as nut butter or white sauce.

Dandelion (Taraxacum officinale)—A low-rating weed in Britain, but cultivated as spinach in the USA, France and

Japan, dandelions contain almost as much vitamin A and C as oranges. Boil them with nettles and sorrel and add a drop of lemon juice—delicious to go with fried bacon. The roots can be washed, chopped and added to stews, or roasted to make coffee.

Fat Hen (Chenopodium album)—Its history as human food goes back to Neolithic man in Europe. The leaves are good raw or cooked, and superb with sweet and sour sauce. The shiny black seeds taste like buckwheat and can be coarse-ground into porridge meal.

Good King Henry (Chenopodium bonus henricus)—Looks like Fat Hen with broader leaves. The whole plant except the root is edible. The peeled stalks and young shoots can be cooked as asparagus (see p. 145), the leaves as spinach. The flower spike is recommended as a vegetable.

Nettle (Urtica diocia)—You can eat stinging nettles, dead nettles or archangels (the yellow ones) and it's stinging nettles which taste best. The sting vanishes when the plant is cooked. Gypsies recommend nettles as a spring tonic for cleansing the blood. A popular recipe is to cook them in a little water, then add some oatmeal and cook for five minutes more. Drain, then add bits of fried bacon and onion, seasoning and spice, and mix well, bind with egg, shape into flat cakes and bake or fry.

Sea beet (Beta maritima)—is found in coastal marshes. Use the young top leaves chopped in salad or cooked as spinach. There are about seventeen kinds of beet; many have edible turnip-like tuberous roots.

Sorrel (Rumex acetosa)—Also called Sour Sauce or Gipsy's Baccy, it is common in meadows and woods. Use only the young spring leaves. They are generally too bitter to eat raw though country folk used to chew the raw leaves as a thirst-quencher. Sorrel is best used to make spring soups, or softened with a white sauce and tomatoes. Before lemons were common it was a regular accompaniment to fish.

Okra (*Hibiscus esculentus*)—has been cultivated for thousands of years in Egypt and grows in tropical and warm temperate regions. The leaves make good spinach. Its unripe seed-pods may be boiled and pulverised to make a glutinous thickener for soups and stews, or can also be eaten like asparagus. The ripe seeds make a good coffee substitute.

Rampion (*Phyteume tenerum*)—grows worldwide. The leaves can be eaten raw in salad or boiled as spinach and the roots taste good raw or cooked as well.

Amaranth—cultivated by the Aztecs, it grows in Africa, Asia and the Americas. It makes excellent spinach, best picked at seeding time.

Asparagus-type Vegetables
Sometimes the stems need peeling before cooking. Cook upright if possible, in a little salted water, simmering for 10 to 15 minutes. Then dip them in butter and eat with your fingers.

Bulrush (*Typha latifolia, T. augustifolia*)—In spring look for the new leaves, grip the inner ones and pull them up; they'll slip free of the roots. The lower white part is good chopped raw in salad. The young roots taste sweet and crunchy. Pull one root (rhizome) and a number will come up. The bulb-like growths are also edible. Keep them moist or they will dry out. Gather the flower-spikes and eat like corn-on-the-cob, frying them first briefly in butter. Even the yellow pollen, which appears after flowering, can be shaken off and used as flour. It's nice mixed in with pancakes or fritter batter.

Burdock (*Arctium majus, A. minus, A. lappa*)—grows wild in Britain, Europe, Asia and North America, it is generally found on the verges of woods, fields and roads. The sturdy stems are best eaten before the plant flowers. Cut the stems low down, peel and simmer until tender. The young leaves can be boiled or steamed. The young shoots are good in salad.

Marsh Samphire (Salicornia europaea)—is a small plant with a succulent house plant look to its oddly angled bulbous stems. It grows in coastal salt marshes round Britain, Europe and the USA. The traditional way of eating samphire is to cut the whole plant and cook it in unsalted water, then hold it by the base and dip in melted butter and strip off the leaves and fleshy stem covering with your teeth.

Bamboo shoots—are not just for giant pandas. Pick them young and up to not more than 20 in (½ m) high. Throw them in the fire embers for ten minutes, then strip off the outer burnt sheath. They're delicious.

Celery-type Vegetables

Alexanders (Smyrnium olusatrum)—grow on damp ground in Britain, Europe and the USA. The whole plant smells like celery and looks a bit like wild celery. Cut the stems back to the ground since the juiciest bit is at the base. Peel and wash. In spring young leaves can be mixed in salads or cooked as spring greens. The closed flower buds are good when cooked for 5 minutes and mixed in salads. You can roast the roots like parsnips, or add them to soup.

Fennel (Foeniculum vulgare)—thrives near sea coasts in open grassy spaces in Britain, Europe, temperate Asia and America. It can grow as tall as a man. Greek athletes ate fennel to give them stamina. Use the bulbous fleshy leaf bases raw or cooked. The young stems can be eaten like asparagus. Use the leaves for flavouring fish. Burning a few fennel stalks on a fire where fish is roasting will impart the flavour to the food. The seeds are reputed to cure depression.

Parsnip-type Vegetables

Salsify (Tragopogon pratensis, T. porrifolius)—grows along verges and in open places in the UK, Europe and America. Peel the roots and fry or roast them. The young leaves and spring shoots may be eaten raw or cooked and the flower stalks can be treated like asparagus.

The Alternative Potato
Carbohydrates (starchy and sugary foods) provide our bodies with daily energy and should constitute about half our intake of food. The other half should be divided between protein, oils and vitamins. To us in the West, potatoes are one of our main sources of carbohydrate, as rice is in the East, but in the tropics they are expensive and seldom available, while the alternatives are very often more nutritious and equally tasty. Boil, bake, roast, fry or mash them like potatoes.

Yams and taro—these are the most universally popular. There are over a hundred varieties of each; they vary in colour, shape and taste (white, yellow, pink, orange, sweet, bitter, globular, heart-shaped, spiny). The yams I saw at a yam festival in New Guinea were 6 ft (2 m) long, and the longest on record there were double that size. Yam growing is men's work, done in secret, and after being harvested the yams are displayed for all to admire, decorated with feathers and yam-masks or faces.

Cassava—(also called manioc or yuca) is widely eaten in the tropics and equatorial belt, and it is worth knowing that it is poisonous (hydrocyanic acid) unless soaked in water for 48 hours before being cooked. In West Africa the soaked tubers are usually dried then pounded to make meal (fufu or gari) and cooked in a paste with water. It is unappetising, but improves if you boil it with grated coconut or fry it with spinach.

Lilies—In temperate and tropical climates, carbohydrate can be obtained from the edible tubers of some species of waterlilies and reeds. The lance lily, corded lily, white lily, yellow lily, goldband lily, spotless lily, star lily, small-leaved lily, wood lily, and tiger lily are just a few which have edible bulbs. They can be eaten raw or cooked like potato. The lotus or blue waterlily (with blue, scented flowers and leathery leaves) has edible root-stock which is nice roasted and crunchy, and the sacred red lotus of Asia has edible roots, stems and seeds. The tender leaves and unopened flowerbuds of the temperate pond lily (*Hymphoea odorata*) can be eaten in spring. Wash and chop the leaves for cooking in soup and stew or in fritters. There was a London clergyman who ate lily sandwiches with jam for breakfast every day for sixteen years.

The most curious edible tuber I've heard of is the man-root, a wild potato vine whose tuber is similar in size and shape to a man. But it is very difficult to dig up and not particularly tasty.

Marrows or squashes—are another source of carbohydrate. Pick them unripe and boil, bake or fry them before eating. Eat them from their skins. Apple squash looks like an apple, and is delicious if boiled and buttered, while pineapple squash is pineapple shaped and equally tasty. Eating the seeds is said to rid you of worms.

Plantain bananas—grow in the tropics, where they have been eaten since antiquity. Nowadays they are sold in tropical markets. I first bought plantain bananas by mistake thinking they were the ordinary variety, and found them hard, woody and inedible. Then I realised they needed cooking. They are most tasty when greenly unripe, and roasted or boiled as potato.

Sago palm—is another source of carbohydrate and provides the staple diet in parts of the Pacific. However, you can't pick and eat it. When sago palms are felled the villagers go to work pounding the inside of the trunk, and washing and straining the pith to extract its edible starch. This is dried into coarse sago flour. Some tribes just cook it in hot water, which tastes awful! Others bake thick pancakes of it in clay 'frying pans'. The pancakes taste good and are remarkable for the energy they provide. After a breakfast of fish and a sago pancake, I wouldn't get hunger pangs until late afternoon, despite being active outdoors all day.

Corn (maize)—is the staple diet of many areas, and is worth remembering for its use throughout its season. At first, when the cob is pale and finger-thick, it is delicious chopped raw in salads; when slightly bigger, boil a few to make a vegetable dish (add salt and butter and eat the whole cob). As the corn grows larger and starts turning yellow, the grains can be chewed raw. The ripe cobs may be de-husked and boiled, or roasted and slowly browned over the fire's embers, or else cooked with the husk on. Pull back the husk and remove the silky threads beforehand.

To choose ripe cobs in a market, look for ones with a fresh-green husk and a dark brown silken tassel, a sign of plump grain. In African village markets you're more likely to find corncobs that have been left on the maize plant until the plant withered and died. These cobs look golden and could be mistaken for ripe ones, but they're too old for cooking. I spent 4 hours boiling some, and they were still as hard as iron. Their proper purpose is to be stored for the dry season and treated like legumes, or to be ground into the coarse flour which is widely called mealie meal. The flour is excellent for porridge, and quite good as potato meal. Usually it is simmered in water until it dries to a thick cake.

It was one of the foods that my horse insisted on sharing. He ate raw meal, and cooked, raw or dried corncobs, plus the whole stalk and leaves too.

Wild Fruit and Berries

Often on a long journey I crave sweet things which is just the body's way of saying it needs the energy they supply. Trekking in rough country you can use up about 3,000 calories a day. Use a crooked stick to pull down the higher branches of fruit trees. The fruit at the top is likely to be the best, since it has had the most sunshine. Raw fruit and berries are extra good mixed with muesli, or chopped in salads. For further variety try making fruit kebabs. Use any fruit that is firm enough when cut into bite-sized pieces or segments and not too ripe. Skewer an assortment of pieces on a long peeled stick to toast quickly over the fire. Brush with honey and lemon, or brown sugar and orange juice, or sugar and melted butter. If you have nutmeg or cinnamon sprinkle a little of that, too. Roast for 5 to 10 minutes turning several times until the baste has crystallised.

Tropical Profusion

The variety of tropical fruits is quite stunning. Indeed, there are about two hundred different kinds of passion fruit on record, and about seventy varieties of banana, ranging from finger-sized red ones to Radjah bananas over a foot long.

Wild mangoes—they are superb, but it'll take you hours to get the strings out from between your teeth. While I collected ripe mangoes from the tree, my horse grabbed any that fell to the ground. He was an expert at chewing off the flesh and spitting out the big stone.

Witgatboom tree—This tree found in Africa has cherry-sized fruit which are very sweet, and its roots may be pounded to make porridge or coffee, or boiled for syrup.

Baobab tree—Readily identifiable by its strange bloated appearance, looking as if it was planted upside-down, the young fruit contains a mushy white substance like cream of tartar which goes well with fish. The mature fruit is rich in vitamin C and can be diluted to make a drink. Inside the fruit are seeds which are invigorating to suck, or they may be roasted and ground to make coffee. The young leaves can be added to meat stews or cooked as a vegetable.

Pawpaw, or papaya—This is found all over the tropics and apart from its delicious fruit (nicest with a squeeze of lime or lemon), its juice is an excellent tenderiser for tough meat, while the leaves may be used for tobacco. The fruit seeds are good for an upset stomach and the fruit skin helps to heal cuts and sores.

Coconut palm—A prime example of the way plants lend themselves to a multitude of uses, its name in Sanskrit, *Kalpa Vriksha* means 'the tree which provides all that is necessary in life'. Its young coconuts give milk, the older ones have nutritious flesh which is tasty raw and superb grated into meat stews; the tender leaf-buds are known as Millionaire's Salad, delicious raw, or they can be cooked as palm cabbage with fish or meat. The tree's branches can be used for roof-thatching, woven into sleeping mats, baskets, fish-bags, and sandals; the leaf-fibres are turned into rope; and leaf-stems make hut walls and arrow-shafts.

Wine may be tapped from the palm's trunk (gouge a hole and stick a bottle in by the neck). Fresh palm wine is like lemonade, refreshing not intoxicating. But it ferments in a few days and becomes highly intoxicating. Salt is also obtained from the trunk, by burning it and boiling the ash. And all this is just from one of the many varieties of palm. Sago palms (see Chapter 16), oil palms, date palms all contribute their own specialities too.

Nut Butter
To make nut-butter or nut-cream, put some shelled roasted nuts into a metal container, add a little water, and use a stone to crush and pound the nuts until they make a smooth paste. It goes well with bread and cookies, or mixed with spinach instead of cream, and on fruit.

Chewing Gum
Some Hottentots and Bushmen of Southern Africa eat a gum extracted from the acacia tree which is reputed to be highly nutritious. Six ounces (170 g) of it will support a man for twenty-four hours.

Mushrooms
There are said to be about 2,000 varieties of edible fungus in the world (roughly two hundred of which grow in the British Isles).

Wild mushrooms need slightly more cooking than cultivated ones, since they are tougher. The simplest way to cook them is upside-down on the fire's embers; use their stalks as a handle, and put some salt and butter (or butter-flavoured salt) in their caps. Cook them until they're toasted brown underneath, and eat them hot. Dried mushrooms are light and useful supplies to carry.

Seaweed

Seaweeds are highly nutritious, rich in vitamins and minerals, especially iodine. They are best when gathered in spring and early summer since, like all plants, they then produce fresh growth which gets tougher as it ages, and dies back during winter.

Do not take seaweed from potentially polluted places. And don't bother using seaweed which is already broken from its hold-fast disc, since it is tough and nutritionally fairly worthless.

Kelp is good boiled with brown rice or chopped up in a white sauce. In parts of South Wales they know all about laver which is traditionally boiled to a black purée, then fried with cockles and bacon. The Japanese grate their seaweed raw and also market it as instant soup. Carrageen moss from the south and west of Ireland can be boiled with milk and lemon and sugar to set as a blancmange. You can also chew it dried, and in Canada dried seaweed is used as a chewing tobacco substitute.

16 *Improvisations and Alternatives*

If you are rolling along in the comparative luxury of your camper van you can pamper your palate by laying in the ingredients for sweet and sour sauce or an apple pie. But even the best stocked travelling households are occasionally down to their last half cup of sugar with no next door neighbour to go to for a refill within a hundred miles. While if you are carrying everything on your back you too will certainly welcome some idea of how you can improvise general cooking ingredients along your way. If you're travelling by van, a book to help you identify indigenous trees and plants and fruits is well worth the space beside the dictionary. If not, try to mug up on some of the following useful flora before you leave home.

Pass the Sugar

Maple syrup—there are several kinds of maple tree in North America, Europe and the Far East, all with sweet sap, though the sugar maple (*Acer saccharinum*) is the best. Cut a groove in the bark and stick a splinter of wood at the bottom of the groove to act as a spout. Put a bowl to catch the sap.

To make syrup you need to evaporate most of the liquid out of the sap. This is time-and-fuel-consuming, but not difficult. Just keep the liquid boiling in an uncovered pot on the fire. The more liquid that evaporates, the thicker and sweeter the syrup.

The Turkish oak (*Quercus cerris*) of Europe and Asia is attacked in summer by small white insects that burrow into the trunk. Sweet sap dribbles out from the holes and forms crystals on the bark. The French tamarisk (*Tamarix gallica*) is a shrub which oozes sweet juice when cut. The

153

flowering ash, or manna ash (*Fraxinus ornus*) produces sweet sap in warm temperate climates which can be collected and treated like maple syrup.

Sugar beet—has sugary juice in its bloated taproot. Boil it down to syrup.

Flowers—follow the principle of 'Where the bee sucks, there suck I'. Cowslip bells are rare but lime flowers are plentiful and positively taste of nectar. Boil the flowers in a little water in a pot without a lid.

Milkweed or silkweed (*Asclepias syriaca*) of North America and Europe has flowers which are used to make a very good brown sugar. The honey flower (*Melianthus major*) of temperate climates has long spikes of dark-brown flowers which are rich in nectar and make excellent syrup. The sugar bush (*Protea mellifera*) has flowers which are used in South Africa for syrup. Honey locust (*Gleditschia triacanthos*) of Europe and North America has seedpods whose sweet pulpy interior can be used for sugar.

Berries and fruit—There are of course innumerable ripe, edible berries and fruits which can be stewed and evaporated to make jammy syrup. In tropical Africa, there is the miraculous berry (*Sideroxylon dulcificum*). Once eaten, its sweetness lingers on in your mouth, making bitter things taste good.

Sweet mastic and sweet African olive have fruits which when ripe are used to sweeten things. These must be used instantly after picking as they will not keep.

Sugar cane—Tear off the outer woody stem and chew the juicy inner, or use it in cooking. I like to get an extra length of sugar cane and use it as a walking stick, but it isn't easy to resist the temptation to nibble the top end. And before I've gone far the walking stick has got so short that to use it I'd have to walk with bent knees.

Sugar palms can be tapped for sweet sap; sweet millet may be boiled down to thick syrup; and sweet hemp (of South America) contains a glucose called Estevin which is 150 times sweeter than sugar.

In scrub desert the camel-thorn (*Alhagi maurorum*) has sugary crystals of sun-scorched sap on its branches. Shake the twigs over a cloth.

Honey—is of course a marvellous sweetener. But it is not simple to find or gather in the bush. However, to smoke out a wild hive, light a smoky fire and direct the smoke into the bees' nest and retreat. Ten minutes of smoking should be enough.

Cooking Oils

Lard, bacon fat, and beef or mutton dripping are of course all excellent for food frying, though dripping may spit a little. Fat may also be rendered down from pieces of animal fat; pork is usually the most suitable. The best fat comes from around the sides of the belly, and beside the ribs. Cut it into small pieces. Put them in a pot with some boiling water; leave the pot uncovered and simmer it gently, stirring occasionally, for about an hour. The lower the heat, the smoother the lard will be. When the pot cools, the globs of fat can be strained off. Scrape away the impurities, and melt the fat in a dry pot, uncovered, to evaporate any remaining water. Re-strain. Farmers sometimes use the pig's bladder (well washed) as a convenient pot for storing the lard.

Other sources of fat—Waterfowl usually have a good layer of fat beneath their skin.

Insects such as flying ants, grasshoppers and locusts contain quantities of oily fat, which comes out when you cook the insects in a dry pan.

Cooking oil from plants—Coconuts will produce oil if you leave their flesh to sweat in the sun.

Palm oil is extracted from the nuts of the oil palm by boiling the nuts for several hours then squeezing them in your hands.

Olive oil, the gourmet's choice, is forced out of the olives by pressing. If you fill a collander with olives, and press them down hard with a plate or flat stone, you should have moderate success.

All types of edible nut such as beech, walnut and almond contain oil. First pound the nuts or chop them roughly, then boil them slowly in water for about two hours, and skim the oil off into a bowl. Alternatively, beech nuts can be roasted, ground and crushed, and walnuts are often crushed for their oil.

Peanuts yield very good oil, obtainable by pounding and boiling.

The cotton plant (*Gossypium berbaceum*) of the tropics, has seeds which are pressed to give good cooking oil or an alternative butter, while the leftover press-mush may be roasted and re-ground for coffee.

In tropical Africa and Asia the seeds of ramtil (*Guizotia abyssinica*) are crushed for oil, which is mild and sweet, usable for salads and cooking, or as a burning oil for fire or light.

Sesame seeds come from the tropical plant, *Sesamum indicum*. Their oil is high quality, suitable for salads or cooking. The press-cake may be used afterwards for baking.

Butter Trees
I've heard of two species of tree that yield 'butter'. The butter tree (*Butyrospermum parkii*) of tropical and equatorial Africa (where it is called Meepampa) yields a sort of butter from the nuts inside its fruit.

Another tropical butter tree (*Combretum butyrosum*) has a buttery fat (called Chiquito in South America) which can be extracted from the fruit.

Flour Substitutes
Not having any shop-style flour doesn't prevent you from baking, if you can find a substitute. Flour may be home-made from innumerable types of grains and seeds, the most popular being wheat, barley, oats, rye, maize, millet, sorghum, buckwheat, quincoa (almost 40 per cent protein, but bitter-tasting unless soaked overnight before

drying and crushing), Inca wheat (originally milled by the Incas), and Amaranth grain (used for flour since the days when Aztec emperors received yearly tributes of this grain).

Any grass seeds can be turned into flour, as so can roots of plants such as arrowroot, lilies, potatoes and breadfruit.

Gather the ripe dry grains, dry them by the fire, and remove the husks by rubbing the grains together in your hands, or crushing them coarsely between stones. Winnowing, which is getting rid of the husks, is traditionally done on a windy day. Pour the crushed grain from hip-height down on to a large spread cloth, and as the grain falls the wind should blow away the husks. Then crush what's left more thoroughly into coarse flour (meal). While travelling, you are likely to find various types of coarse flour for sale in marketplaces, which can add interesting and tasty flavours to your baking.

Ways to Obtain Salt

If you run out of salt while near the sea, you may find dry deposits along the shore and on tidal flats. Otherwise, take a large pan of sand-free seawater and keep it boiling (without a lid) over a fire until all the water has evaporated.

A salty flavour is also produced by boiling in sea water, or cooking food wrapped in seaweed.

Away from the sea, people used to obtain salt from natural inland salt springs or brine wells. In some remote places this is still common practice. In New Guinea I went with a group of village-women to their local salt spring, six miles distant. We took parcels of dried out banana-tree fibre, and at the springs we spread the fibre to soak up the brine (salt water). After carrying the saturated fibre back to the village it was put in the sun to dry, evaporating the water and keeping the salt.

Alternatively, hickory and palm trees are sometimes burnt to ashes, and the ashes are boiled to make black-coloured salt.

Lemon Substitutes

Apart from shop items such as concentrated lemon, lemon powder (for drinks), and citric acid, a lemon flavour may also be obtained from certain plants.

Lemon mint, lemon verbena, lemon balm and lemon thyme (smaller than common thyme with rich evergreen foliage), are sometimes used to give lemon flavour in cookery. Best cooked with fish, veal, or poultry. Don't use a large amount, just one or two sprigs lying on the meat, or chopped up finely in a stuffing or sauce. They are nice too in salads and fruit stews.

Sorrel and dock leaves can add a sharp lemon tang to white meat or spring puddings.

Things like Tomatoes

The tree-tomato is an elongated fruit which tastes very similar to an ordinary tomato; the tree grows worldwide in warm climates.

There are also strawberry tomatoes, cherry tomatoes, ground tomatoes, currant tomatoes and grape tomatoes.

The most common tropical alternatives are the cherry tomato (*Alkekengi*), or dwarf Cape gooseberries. A good sauce may be made from the berries, or cook them mixed with other vegetables. The tropical sun berry, the American pepino, the children's tomato of Africa, and the Polynesian fidgi tomato may be cooked to make tomato-like soups and sauces.

The diverse fruits of the Pacific islands include one which is acclaimed as tomato sauce by white settlers, and was traditionally eaten at cannibal feasts by the islanders.

Garlic Breath

Garlic grows wild and cultivated throughout the temperate world, and has been used in flavouring for at least 2,000 years. Various wild leeks also provide a mild garlic flavour, like the sand leek which has bulbs in its stem and underground.

Garlicwort or sauce-alone (*Sisymbrium alliaria*) of

Europe and Asia, has leaves which go well in salads and sauces. The leaves should be picked before the plant flowers.

Bank cress or hedge mustard was formerly used in Europe instead of garlic. Chop or purée the leaves in sauces.

For a garlic onion flavour, try garlic mustard.

Almost as Keen as Mustard

Mustard flavour may be found in the crushed seeds of the mustard tree (*Salvadora persica*) in warm temperate climates. The shoots and young leaves are good in salads or meat sauces. The red berries are also edible.

Coffee of a Sort

Chicory is the most well-known coffee substitute. It is believed to be slimming, and is also popular for its lack of tannic acid and caffeine. It tastes bitter but flavoursome. Use the roots, roasted and ground.

Other roots which may be used as coffee substitutes are those of dandelions (pleasant-tasting, and supposed to ease stomach pains and indigestion); or of quackgrass, or skirret.

Don't bother looking for big fat roots, since they only take longer to bake and need to be chopped up. Wash and scrub the roots well, then let dry. Put them in tinfoil and roast them in the fire's grey embers (medium-hot) until they're baked dry brown (about 30 minutes), or leave the roots beside the fire all night to become brittle. After they've cooled, grind them to coarse powder. If you have no grinder, put them in a cloth and hammer them to bits between rocks. Bake the grounds for 10 to 15 minutes more, until dark brown not charred black.

Allow 2 tablespoons of very coarsely ground coffee per mug of water. The boiling water should be added to the coffee in a pot, then covered and left to soak for an hour. (The smaller the grounds, the less time they need to soak.) Re-heat before drinking.

Tisane

A tisane, or herbal tea, is made by adding boiling water to certain flowers or leaves in a pot. Then cover the pot and leave it in a warm place to infuse (brew) for 5 to 10 minutes.

For a stronger tisane, bruise or chop up the herbs to make them release more flavour, and simmer them in the water for a few minutes before brewing. Some tisanes taste less good on their own but all right when mixed half-and-half with ordinary tea. Try combining and blending different tisanes (clover and camomile are delicious together).

I like to add a pinch of ginger to tea. Another favourite is to brew it with mixed spices and bring it to the boil with milk (an Indian tradition).

Cow Trees

Fresh milk is obtained from cows, goats, sheep, mares and camels. In dry scrubland the cows yield little, and it is sometimes made into a sort of yoghourt by adding urine and fresh blood. If you don't mind the idea, you'll find the taste is refreshing.

Milk may also be obtained from certain plants. The cow tree (*Mimusops elata*) of South America has apple-sized fruit which contain thick creamy milk. It is almost indistinguishable from real cow's milk, and it goes well in coffee. It looks fresh and foamy, but if left standing it quickly begins to get gluey and solid.

The milk tree (*Brosium galactodendron*) of South America and Asia is described by the pioneer, Humboldt:

On the barren flank of a rock grows a tree with coriaceous and dry leaves. Its large, woody roots can scarcely penetrate into the stone. For several months of the year not a single shower moistens its foliage. Its branches appear dead and dried; but when the trunk is pierced there flows from it a sweet and nourishing milk. It is at the rising of the sun that this vegetable fountain is most abundant. The natives are seen hastening from all quarters, furnished with large bowls to receive the milk which grows yellow and thickens at its surface. Some empty their bowls under the tree itself, others carry the juice home to their children.

Bearing the name milk, the juice inside unripe coconuts is plentiful, cool and nourishing.

Fresh or dried milk produced from soy beans is sold in many countries, as are powdered milk or concentrated pellets of dried milk which can be very useful.

Stopgap Tobacco
For a smoker there are few things worse than running right out of tobacco. I've run out many times in remote places, and been reduced to trial-and-error tactics with a variety of leaves (most tasted sickly and made me cough), and dried grasses (which burn too hot), but I still didn't give up smoking!

In temperate climates I discovered that coltsfoot (*Tussilago farfara*) is a popular tobacco substitute. The plant can be recognised by its yellow dandelion-like flowers on thick reddish scaly stems; the flowers appear before the leaves in spring, and turn into fluffy seed-clocks. When the leaves come, they're large, hoof-shaped, and furry underneath.

Coltsfoot's botanical name means cough-remedy. For centuries in Europe the leaves were smoked as a cure for bronchitis and lung complaints. Nowadays it's a major ingredient of manufactured herbal tobacco. Other leaves which are added to smoking mixtures are mullein, bearberry, betony, bogbean, camomile and eyebright.

In the tropics, pawpaw (papaya) leaves are the most common tobacco substitute. There are others—ask the old men of a village to show you the plants.

With small leaves, I used to dry them by the fire, and when they were crisp, crumble them and fill a pipe for smoking. (For two years in Africa I smoked a pipe made out of a rolled twist of metal off a wrecked Land Rover in a desert. It was special to me because it was made by a metal-smith who rode a white racing camel.)

If rolling tobacco in paper, the paper will keep flaring into flame unless you rub and crinkle it to break up the fibres. Newspaper is good, it is not hot and it burns correctly.

In Nigeria the locally made roll-up is called 'bookie', named after the Good Book given by the early missionaries to people who discovered that the Bible's superfine pages were excellent as cigarette papers.

Large tobacco or substitute leaves give a better smoke if dried slowly for a few months, though I'm satisfied with drying them just for a few days. They should be hung in bunches by their stalks in a warm airy place. The closest I could get to that was to hang the leaves from a string between poles in my canoe, but if I had a lot of leaves they caught the wind and pushed the canoe off course, which was a novel sort of smoking hazard. Every evening I'd hang them to absorb the smoky flavours of the fire.

When they're crisply dry, scrunch them to bits. You can smoke a leaf before it's completely dry by rolling it up as a thick cigar. Tobacco leaves like this are excellent.

Tobacco leaves are worth carrying as trade items or gifts. Stored leaves should be tightly packed. Loose crumbled tobacco may be bought in bush marketplaces for a few cents per handful. It's full of twigs and pebbles, rough smoking, but I smoked it happily for years. Chewing tobacco is preferred in some countries, and can also be bought in the markets.

Toothpaste and Twigs
Fresh strawberries are reputed to remove brown stains from teeth. They also dissolve tartar and strengthen the gums. The trick is to remember to keep rubbing them against your teeth long enough and not just to enjoy swallowing them straight down. Raspberries may be used in the same way, but they're not as effective as strawberries.

Toothpaste is a fairly modern invention, and probably more than half the world's population have never used it. If tribesmen catch sight of you brushing your teeth they look amazed, or sometimes terrified because they think you're foaming at the mouth with rabies! In villages, people cluster round to see what you're doing—it is disconcerting to have a crowd of onlookers watching you brush your teeth.

These people generally chew the twigs of certain trees and shrubs, though often without realising that the twigs are cleaning their teeth, gums, and destroying germs. Different places use different trees. The best-known are the cinnamon tree (chew a small piece of the bark, which is hot-tasting but effective); and the mastic tree. Cut a groove in the tree trunk to extract the resin, or mastic. Dry it to gum before use, then chew to clean and freshen your mouth. Alternatively, brush your teeth with the powdered leaves of marjoram, or the powdered roots of mallow, or powdered bark from the plum tree, all of which are good for teeth and gums.

Fennel stalks, parsley and sage are used to cure bad breath and to freshen the mouth. Chew a young raw stem. Raw sorrel and other tangy leaves will freshen your palate.

Alternative Soaps

A good soap may be made by boiling the roots of the flowering yucca plant. Boil them hard to extract the juices; use the syrup as soap. The pink soapwort plant yields a soapy juice that is effective against grease. Wild basil, camomile, or elderflowers may be used to make fragrant washing water.

Holding It All Together

Rope—anyone who's watched a Tarzan film will have a vague idea about doing things with vines or creepers when you run out of that essential but space-consuming commodity, rope. This is how to cut a piece of leather or rawhide to make a thong. Start by cutting a large circle, continuing cutting in decreasing spirals inwards, like a watchspring, and make it supple by tying one end to a tree branch, putting a stick through the other end, and twisting the stick to wring the thong in both directions. One an inch wide is enough for a horse tether.

String—Some seaweeds have fronds which look like rope and grow up to 40 ft (13 m) long. When half dry, the skin is peeled off and twisted to make string. The outer bark of some trees, or the stems of many plants will make fibrous string. To make the fibres hold together properly you twist the string in one direction and roll it with your hand (easiest against your leg) in the other direction. When pulled, the string fibre should re-twist properly.

　　Other string options include a few hairs from a horse's tail, not twisted but braided.

Thread—can be made from the long strips of outer membrane which you peeled off the intestine of an animal after soaking. The membrane should be twisted and hung to dry. Strips of sinews can be used for thread by twisting or braiding them. Let the whole sinew dry before pulling strips off it, then wet the strips and scrape them smooth. They say it is easiest done with your teeth. Then twist and rub the strip with your hand to prevent fraying.

Glue—is produced if you boil up animal hide or hooves without charring them, until they yield liquid. For emergency improvisation, it is worth knowing that horn can be boiled in water or heated until it gets soft enough to mould into different shapes. It is also possible to weld two pieces of horn by heating and pressing the edges together.

17   Health and First Aid

When taken ill in the Third World, don't automatically assume that any European doctor is going to be a good doctor. Remember the awful stories of doctors barred for malpractice at home who set up private clinics in faraway places, and do as you would in Europe, try to see a doctor recommended by someone who's used him and lives to tell the tale. On several occasions during my travels I've been treated by witch doctors. Some throw bones (old knuckle bones) to diagnose the sickness; others use less definable methods. The experience is always worthwhile and the treatments are usually herbal.

In the Congo forest when I had severe bronchitis I was taken to a witch doctor so old that his dark skin hung in loose folds down his skinny chest, and his bald head was crowned by a few white popples of hair. I paid him the sum of two chickens. We sat down on a mat and he played a kind of sitar until he was lost in a trance. A calabash of water was brought to him and he threw some brown twigs into it; the water immediately started to bubble.

Around us people were dancing and chanting, but the witch doctor and I seemed held in limbo; his serenity was almost tangible. The water fizzed until it was seething. I was given a mugful to drink, which tasted bubbly and bitter. At the end the doctor filled two old beer-bottles with the twigs and liquid, and told me that I must drink both bottles every day; and refill them every day, until the time that the water no longer fizzed. On that day, the cure would be complete.

Whatever it was, it definitely put me on the mend, though complete recovery was slow.

If you are travelling by camper van you can equip

yourself with the basic first-aid kit mentioned in Chapter 2. Even if you don't use a pill or a plaster, it can help you make friends along the way. Here now are some basic do's and don'ts for instant emergencies and these are followed by a convenient table of herbal remedies for further treatment. For, of course, these tried and tested decoctions, infusions and poultices have been with us always and are there along your route for the gathering.

Foot Problems
To prevent blisters, put soap on the inside of your socks before setting out. To soften shoe-leather, break a raw egg into your boot before putting it on.

Stomach Ailments
Prevention is better than cure; build immunity to germs. One cannot expect to come straight from sterile Western food to Third World market cooking without ill effects. Immunity to most minor germs is gained by letting your digestive system get used to less pure food (like the water) in a gradual way.

Even so, I keep these rules: wash or peel uncooked food and fruit; avoid drinking ice, it is frequently made from impure water; remember to wash your hands before eating; don't eat under-cooked meat.

Drink plenty of water, it flushes bugs through your system. It is also important to drink plenty when you're ill, especially with fever, flu, or diarrhoea. The best cure for diarrhoea is starvation and plenty of water. If you must eat, stick to broth or rice and rice water.

Frostbite
Get yourself out of freezing places before you start treatment. Repeated warming and re-freezing makes it worse. Thaw the afflicted part gradually in luke-warm water or, failing that, in a friend's armpit. Don't massage to restore circulation. That does more harm than good. The process must be gradual.

Hypothermia and Exposure

Hypothermia is dangerous because once you have it you don't realise anything is wrong, and your judgment is affected, often in critical mountain situations. It occurs when the body temperature has dropped too low. If it goes eight degrees below normal you can die. So when you find yourself stumbling, shivering, feeling tired and uncaring, stop and make a hot drink, wrap yourself in some blankets or more clothes and decide about making camp. Hot drinks, shelter, warmth and rest for 48 hours are the treatment for recovery.

Heat Stroke

For heat exhaustion the best remedy is salt water, one teaspoon of salt to 1¾ pints (1 litre) of water. In a small pearl-fishers' village off the coast of the Thai peninsula, many of the girls painted their faces with white powder (like talc) mixed with water, and while I lived with them they painted my face white, too. This reflected the sun away from the skin. It certainly stopped my face getting burnt, quite an achievement since we spent most days out on the sea in a canoe. The sea was irresistible, dotted with hundreds of little sheer-sided humpy islands, with pinnacles and solitary columns of oddly-eroded rock. But I had a fright every time I caught sight of my reflection in the water!

Burns

Shut out the air immediately, either by placing the burnt part in cold water for 5 to 10 minutes, or by wrapping it in a clean cloth. Don't break burn blisters as they protect the wound from infection.

Fever

One treatment recommends dulling the fever and reducing the temperature by taking aspirin. The other, which I believe in, is sweating it out. You pile on extra blankets and drench everything in sweat for 24 hours. Quinine, the standard treatment for malaria, comes from the bark of the South American cinchona tree.

How to Control Bleeding

Raise the injured part. Press your hand or a clean cloth over the wound, and keep pressing until bleeding stops. This generally takes 15 minutes.

Use a cloth tourniquet in extreme circumstances, tied above the injury. Loosen the tourniquet every 20 minutes.

Healing Wounds

Pioneers in Africa noted that red ants can be used to close a deep cut, by holding the ant's body so that its pincers bite into both sides of the cut skin.

The danger of any small open wound in the tropics is that it easily gets infected and becomes a tropical ulcer, which looks revolting and is quite difficult to cure. Clean the wound of all white pus, keep it dry and covered. Sea water, if available, is excellent for cleaning wounds. When the skin around the sore loses its redness, the infection has gone away.

Plants have been used in healing wounds from the earliest days. Yarrow used to be carried into battle to staunch blood flow. It also has antiseptic qualities. Achilles used it during the siege of Troy and it was still being carried by soldiers in the Second World War. Bloodwort, staunchwound and allheal have names which proclaim their properties. They operate by closing the capillaries.

Broken Bones

Don't let the broken ends get moved about, unless they're in a bad position, in which case, the sooner they're set right, the better they'll mend. Make a splint of wood, wrap the broken limb to it in a sleeve of tree bark.

To improvise a plaster cast, you need to find a plant which produces the type of sap that sets hard and firm without irritating the skin. The Mexicans know how to use a tree-climbing arum lily, *Solda con Solda* and a plant from the bean family, the Tepeguaje. This is their method for making a cast of Tepeguaje:

Put 2¼ lb (1 kg) of bark into 10 pints (5 litres) of water

and boil it until most of the water has evaporated, leaving a thick syrup. Dip some strips of cloth in the syrup and get ready to bind them around the broken limb. It's wise to put a soft dry cloth directly on the skin and a layer of raw cotton or kapok fluff, before wrapping the syrup-cloth around to make a cast that is firm but not tight. The broken limb may swell, and if the cast gets too tight it will have to be cut off and replaced more loosely. The cast should cover far above and below the break to stop it moving. Never put a cast on an open wound.

The temperate herb comfrey is also known in Europe as Boneset or Knitbone. Use poultices of freshly bruised leaves.

Dislocations

Try to put the bone back into place as soon as possible. If it doesn't stay in place, bandage it or use a sling. To re-set a dislocated shoulder, find a raised surface where the injured person can lie flat, face down, with the dislocated arm hanging towards the ground with enough clearance for him to hold a bucketful of stones in his hand for ten minutes. At the end of this time the joint should pop back into place when the weighted bucket is released. If you don't have a convenient raised surface, lay the victim on his back on the ground and lie down beside him, facing the other way round, so you can put you bare foot into his armpit. Pull the arm slowly down at an angle of about forty-five degrees to the body, using a steady pull for ten minutes. Then move the arm closer to the body, using your foot to position the bone. The joint should slip back into place.

Bruises, Strains and Sprains

To reduce swelling, raise the injured part and keep it raised.

Treat Yourself Herbal

The emphasis so far has been on first aid. But herbal remedies have been around for centuries and there are literally thousands of them. The following pages give you the chance to sample a small selection and cure your own ills in time-tested ways. Remember, people react in different ways to different plants and a lot depends on the original cause of infection.

Herbal remedies can be administered in various ways, internally or externally. I have used the following terminology in the table:

Decoction   approximately a handful of pounded and crushed leaves, boiled down and applied externally

Tea   quantity as for a strong pot of tea, but less boiled down than a decoction, and taken internally

Compress   substances mashed, pulped, grated or bruised to a juicy consistency and applied between two pieces of mosquito netting, if you've nothing better

Poultice   a heated version of a compress

TOOTHACHE	cloves	suck cloves
	yarrow	chew leaves
	plantain	leaf tea as mouthwash
	mallow, marsh mallow	powdered root as mouthwash
SWOLLEN GUMS	cress	to chew
EYE INJURIES	comfrey, eyebright, camomile, fennel	use decoction as eyewash
	celandine	apply diluted juice (2 tsp in cup of water). But poisonous if taken internally
DIARRHOEA	agrimony, meadowsweet, balm	leaf tea (also seeds of plantain)
	blackberry juice	drink
	sorrel	tea of roots and seeds
	ash	tea of bark

DYSENTERY	bistort	tea of crushed roots
	marsh mallow	tea of roots and leaves
	periwinkle, horsetail, sanicle, loosestrife	leaf tea. Sanicle and loosestrife help stop internal bleeding
	quince	eat raw fruit
BRONCHITIS AND OTHER RESPIRATORY COMPLAINTS	fennel, sanicle, vervain, lungwort, pennyroyal	leaf tea
	marsh mallow	tea from the roots
	honeysuckle	tea from the flowers
	elecampane	inhale a decoction of the roots
	coltsfoot	powder leaves for snuff, or as tea
CHILBLAINS	yarrow, mullein, marsh mallow, walnut	make a compress from crushed leaves
	turnip	crushed and heated as a poultice
SUNBURN	nettles, witchhazel, salad burnet, elderflower or berry	dab on a decoction
	strawberries	crushed
	potato	grated raw as a compress
BURNS	borage, burdock	apply compress of chopped leaves
	ivy	compress of chopped leaves is excellent for restoring injured tissue and as painkiller. But poisonous taken internally
	dead nettle	boil until it jells and apply compress
	aloe-vera	a tropical leaf containing slimy jelly, apply as compress
FEVER	sorrel, borage	leaf tea
	ash	tea from the bark

STOPPING BLEEDING	Alexanders, horsetail, knapweed, yarrow, bloodwort, staunchweed, all-heal	compress or decoction from the crushed leaves
	sloe	a compress from the juice
	walnut	compress from a decoction of the catkins
	cardon cactus	slice off a piece and hold to the wound
HEALING SORES, WOUNDS, STINGS, INFLAMMATION	birch	a compress of crushed leaves, or disinfect the wound with a decoction
	lime	use a decoction of pounded bark as a dressing
	vervain, sage, mallow (sorcerers believed vervain bestowed immortality)	as an infusion or compress
	hogweed	a compress of crushed roots and leaves (also good for impotence and frigidity!)
	aloes (the tropical orange poker variety)	rub the leaf on the sting or bite, as we do docks or plantain at home
BROKEN BONES	comfrey (a local name is knitbone)	poultice of the leaves
BRUISES, STRAINS, SPRAINS	Arnica montana	weak leaf tea
	witchhazel, hyssop, archangels, daisy	decoction or compress
	cabbage	hot leaf poultice

Finally, no chapter on travelling health and welfare would be complete without a morose look at the pests and bloodsuckers which can make a misery of a day's journey and purgatory of the sleepless night.

Flies and Mosquitoes

These can make a beautiful place thoroughly unpleasant.

Chapter 5 gives advice about insect-infested camping spots and how to avoid them. But in certain areas it is impossible to be free of insects. Even the Eskimos have a word for mosquito. Without some insect-repellent you can suffer badly and without a mosquito-net you'd go nearly crazy. If you have no shop-type insect-repellent, you can use natural repellents such as tobacco or elder leaves. Crush the leaves and rub them on your skin. The effects aren't very long-lasting, but bring temporary relief.

People are not chemically identical, and for some people certain repellents don't work, so when you find one that is effective for you, remember what it is.

Your body should give off an insect-repelling odour if you eat quantities of cream of tartar (available also in tablet form), or drink two tablespoons of vinegar in a mug of water. Wine-vinegar and cider-vinegar are less awful-tasting than others. Garlic, eaten or rubbed on your skin, should repel flies. Repellents that you eat or drink should be effective for about 24 hours.

Smoke is a good insect deterrent; put wet leaves and damp wood on the fire. In swampland villages at dusk the people may lay little piles of smoking coconut husks around your feet. Red cedar wood or green ferns are also effective.

Most insects are seasonal. The first rain of the season will bring them out and the wet season (or summer) sees them at their most plentiful. If you time your visits to swampland to coincide with the dryest or coldest seasons, you will encounter few if any insects to disturb your peace. It was the rainy season when I set out paddling a canoe down the Congo river. On the first night I rigged up my mosquito-net in the dugout; there were some mosquitoes inside the net and I killed them. Minutes later I found many more and then I saw why. I stared in shocked fascination. The outside of my net was thickly covered in a layer of mosquitoes, small ones, which simply folded back their wings and crawled through the netting. That river journey took nearly two months. We had no mosquito-repellents, and I can scarcely describe the horror of those long nights.

However, progressing downriver we moved into country where the rainy season had not yet arrived, and at nights I slept lying in the dry sand beside the river's edge, without a mosquito-net. Whenever I opened my eyes in the darkness I could see clearly out over the wide silvery water, banked by the dark shape of primeval rain forest. Silence, with some distant monkeys fighting, but without the howl of insects. It was a kind of paradise.

To Repel Fleas and Lice

Rub yourself with mint. Walnut leaves have similar properties, used freshly crushed, or bath in an infusion to get rid of bugs, fleas, moths, lice and ants.

Tumbo Flies

There are other names for this type and similar tropical flies that lay their eggs on damp clothes spread to dry in the sun. Unless the clothes are ironed, the eggs may transfer to your skin, and you get some terribly itchy swellings which you must not scratch, or they go badly infected. In time a hole appears on the swelling and out will crawl a maggot. To hasten the process you can smear vaseline over the hole; the maggot needs to breathe and will poke its head through, then you squeeze the swelling and it should pop out. To avoid incurring them, don't leave your damp washing by fruit trees.

Jiggers

Jiggers (Chigoe) are like a flea of the rain-forest in Africa and South America. I've heard they are deterred if you eat cream of tartar tablets, or dust your clothes with sulphur, and wearing boots helps.

Jiggers usually go in under your toe nails to lay their eggs. They become very itchy but don't scratch or they'll go rotten. Wait for a few days until they're ripe. I took mine to a village's tame monkey, and it knew what to do. I suppose monkeys also get jiggers. It checked my toes carefully and chattered excitedly when it found the swelling. Taking a splinter of bamboo it gently cut open my skin and hooked out a small opaque bag of eggs. The villagers applauded and said that no one could do it as neatly as a monkey.

Ticks

Ticks bury their heads under your skin while their body swells up with your blood.

If you get covered in ticks, take a bath in kerosene diluted with water, and wash your hair in it. Pepper ticks are so tiny they look like specks of pepper.

Ticks in certain regions of the world can cause tick-bite fever. When pulling a tick off your skin, make sure the head comes out too. If the mark stays for days and turns red with a small black scab, you've probably already got the fever. Go to a doctor for antibiotic treatment.

Where ticks carry fever, don't sleep in the undergrowth. My hammock kept me safe at night, but I got plenty of ticks in the daytime, and the fever followed.

It came so suddenly that I didn't realise I'd got it until a lucid moment during the delirium. I was riding across a wild part of Zululand, and in my determination not to fall off unconscious, I roped myself to my horse's back.

Leeches

Leeches will be found along jungle paths, hanging in foliage overhead and in the undergrowth; they attach themselves to your legs or drop on to you as you pass. (They can lie in wait for up to a year without food.) You won't feel their bite, and they can swell to ½ in (10 mm) before dropping off.

If a leech is crawling on you, scrape it off with a knife-blade. If it is already sucking blood, put salt on it, or burn it with a cigarette to make it drop off. The anti-coagulant it injects while sucking will cause your blood to flow out for a while afterwards, but eventually it should form a clot.

Poisonous Creepy-Crawlies

These include scorpions, hunting spiders, tarantulas, black widows, some centipedes and some snakes. I was once bitten by a hunting spider and it was the most painful and frightening experience of my life. Within a short time my body was paralysed, my throat muscles were almost closed and I gasped for breath. My heart felt like a clenched fist and was hammering as though I'd run up a mountain. I was freezing cold but sweat poured off me, and the pain all through me was mind-boggling. I had no antidote, and it was two weeks before I recovered enough to walk. But this was an exceptional experience. The bites of these poisonous creatures, including many snakes, are very seldom fatal. Their image just suffers from co-starring with the baddie in so many B movies. Generally they will only attack in fear or self-defence, and with a bit of common sense you can take avoiding action.

Always knock empty shoes or boots before putting them on. If walking through tall grass and undergrowth, walk with heavy stamping footsteps to warn creatures to move out of your way. I saw very few snakes and either they have slithered away or they've been asleep. Once, after a rainy night spent sleeping on the ground, I found a snake lying beside me sharing my shelter. It left when I moved. The bite of a non-poisonous snake leaves two superficial rows of teethmarks but no deep fangmark. The bite of a poisonous snake leaves deep marks of two fangs, and sometimes other smaller teethmarks.

If you do get bitten by a poisonous snake and have a chance to reach hospital for a serum injection, it helps to apply an icepack to the bite to slow down the spread of the poison through your system. If you haven't an icepack and can't get to medical treatment, you still have a good chance of survival if you can only manage to stay calm (easier said than done, I know) and don't over-exert yourself. Fear accelerates the heartbeat and pumps the poison along faster. Some people recommend sucking and spitting out the poison. Apply a tourniquet, then cut the wound open with a sterilised knife, cutting on the fangmarks, ½ in (10 mm) long and ¼ in (5 mm) deep. Suck and spit for 15 minutes. A tourniquet is helpful anyway to slow down the flow of poison, but don't tie it so tight it blocks the main arteries. Loosen it for thirty seconds every twenty minutes to prevent gangrene. It's also helpful to drink a lot of water, which dilutes the venom.

But these are measures for extreme circumstances. I don't carry snake-bite serum because I don't foresee a need for it. The likelihood of poisonous bites really is rare and no reason to stop you going where you want to go, provided you take the sensible precautions. Indeed, the more I travel, the more I realise how little there is to fear, and that the worst creepy-crawlie problem you are likely to have to contend with on your journey will probably be the tiny sugar ants that get into your supplies.

Appendix 1: Maps and Guides

US Geological Survey, Branch Distribution—Eastern Region, 1200 South Eads Street, Arlington, VA 22202. For topographical maps east of the Mississippi including Minnesota, Puerto Rico and the Virgin Islands. No phone orders.

US Geological Survey, Branch Distribution—Central Region, Box 25286, Federal Center, Denver, CO 80225. For topographical maps west of the Mississippi, including Alaska, Hawaii, Louisiana, Guam and American Samoa. No phone orders.

Department of Energy, Mines and Resources, Canada Map Office, 615 Booth Street, Ottawa, Ontario, Canada K1A 0E9. (613) 995-3065. For Canadian maps by mail order.

PACIFIC TRAVELLERS SUPPLY, 529 State Street, Santa Barbara, CA 93101. (805) 963-4438. Excellent selection of worldwide maps and guidebooks, including Baedekers, Berlitz, Blue Guides, Fodor's, Frommer's, Let's Go, Lonely Planet, Insight, Michelin, Bartholomew, Falk, Hallwag, Japan Map Guide, Kummerly-Frey, New Zealand Government, Ordnance Survey (Britain), Plan Guide Blay (Italian), Rand McNally, UBD (Australia), USGS. Mail order or walk in.

BRADT ENTERPRISES, Inc, 95 Harvy Street, Cambridge, MA 02140 (617) 492-8776. Mail order house selling maps and a number of guidebooks listed in the bibliography.

ROYAL ROBBINS, 1314 Coldwell Avenue, Modesto, CA 95350 (800) 344-7277, or within California: (800) 336-8661.

Major outdoor travel companies, such as MOUNTAIN TRAVEL, Inc, 1398 Solano Avenue, Albany, CA 94706 (415) 527-8100, occasionally also have a selection of foreign maps and hard to find books.

For a listing of map libraries in the US, write to the SPECIAL LIBRARIES ASSOCIATION, 1700 18th Street NW, Washington DC 20009 (202) 234-4700 for the 4th Edition of
Map Collections in the United States, a 1985 imprint. Price is $35.00.

Overseas map houses: Write early for their catalogs as orders will take time to be shipped.

STANFORD INTERNATIONAL MAP CENTRE, 12–14 Long Acre, London WC2E 9LP, England.

GEO CENTRE, International Landkartenhaus, 7, Stuttgart 80, Vaihingen, Honigiveisenstrasse 25, West Germany.

GEO BUCH, 8000 Munchen 2, Rosenthal 6, West Germany.

LIBRERIA ALPINA, Via C. Coronedi-Berti, 4, 40137 Bologna, Zona 3705, Italy.

Appendix 2: Vehicle Advice

AUTOMOBILE ASSOCIATION OF AMERICA (AAA), 8111 Gatehouse Road, Falls Church, VA 22047 (703) 222-6000, or look in your regional phone book for a local office. The AAA has information and applications for an International Driver's Permit (US Driver's License required). You do not need to be a AAA member to apply. For international rentals, road maps and conditions, carnets de passage and other information concerning travel with vehicles, ask for 'Worldwide Travel' at your local office or call (703) 222-6811.

If you plan to use other, more exotic means of transport, like camels, yaks or horses, and you feel uncomfortable about waiting until you arrive in your destination country to do so, the best alternative is to contact one of the better established adventure travel companies. Because they operate trips in remote areas, they usually have reliable outfitter contacts that may be able to arrange something for you in advance. This method will certainly be more expensive than if you arrange for pack animals yourself by asking local people for assistance. But if you're travelling under time constraints, this may be your only realistic alternative.

Further Reading
The Four Wheel Drive Book, by Jack Jackson, Haynes Publications.
Overland and Beyond, by T. and J. Hewatt, Bradt Enterprises.

Bicycling
National Off Road Bicycle Association (NORBA), 2175 Holly Lane, Solvang, CA, 93463 (805) 688-2325—

Source for information relating to all facets of mountain biking and recreation.

Mountain Bike Manufacturers/Distributors: Since many mountain bikes are constructed of parts made in Japan, probably the easiest way to acquire one is to buy one from a bicycle shop in your area, or the area you plan to travel. All of the manufacturers/distributors listed below sell through dealers around the country. Call or write to get a list of dealers.

FISHER MOUNTAIN BIKES, 1421 East Francisco Blvd, San Rafael, CA 94901 (415) 459-2247.

FUJI AMERICA WEST, 465 California Street, San Francisco, CA 94104 (415) 986-7797.

IBIS CYCLE, PO Box 275, Sebastopol, CA 95472 (707) 829-5615.

RITCHEY USA, Route #2 Box 405, La Honda, CA 94020 (415) 368-4018.

ROSS BICYCLES, 350 Beach 79th Street, Rockaway Beach, NY 11693.

Mail Order Mountain Bike Repair Tools
THE THIRD HAND, 3101 North Old Stage Road, Mt. Shasta, CA 96067 (916) 926-2600.

Appendix 3: Camping Equipment and Health Supplies

Camping Equipment Manufacturers: Many of these companies sell through mail order catalogs. Others will give you a list of dealers that carry their products in your locale. Call or write to them for more information.

ADVENTURE 16, 4620 Alvarado Canyon Road, San Diego, CA 92120 (619) 283-6314.

ALPENLITE, 3891 North Ventura Avenue, Ventura, CA 93001 (805) 653-0431.

ALPINE RESEARCH, Inc, 1930 Central Avenue, Suite F, Boulder, CO 80301 (303) 444-0660.

BRIGADE QUARTERMASTERS LTD, 266 Roswell Street, Marietta, GA 30060 (404) 428-1234.

BUTTERMILK MOUNTAIN WORKS, 2333 North Sierra Highway, Bishop, CA 93514 (619) 872-1946.

CLIMB HIGH, Box 9210 South Burlington, Vermont 05401 (802) 864-4122.

EAGLE CREEK TRAVEL GEAR, PO Box 651, Solana Beach, CA 92075 (800) 874-9925; in CA: (619) 755-9399.

EASTERN MOUNTAIN SPORTS, 1041 Commonwealth Avenue, Boston, MA 02215 (617) 254-4250. EMS no longer produces a catalog, but they will accept mail orders if you know exactly what you need.

EASTPAK, 17 Locust Street, Haverhill, MA 01830 (617) 373-7581.

EDDIE BAUER, PO Box 3700, Seattle, WA 98124 (800) 426-8020.

JANSPORT, Paine Field Industrial Park, Building 306, Everett, WA 98204 (206) 353-0200.

JOHNSON CAMPING/EUREKA TENTS/CAMP TRAILS, PO Box 966, Binghampton, NY 13903 (607) 723-7546.

KELTY PACK COMPANY, 118 Industrial Road, New Haven, MO 63068 (314) 237-4427.

LATOK MOUNTAIN GEAR, PO Box 380, Lyons, CO 80540 (303) 823-5530.

L. L. BEAN, Inc, Freeport, ME 04033 (800) 221-4221.

LOWE ALPINE SYSTEMS, PO Box 189, Lafayette, CO 80026 (303) 665-9220.

MADDEN USA, 2400 Central Avenue, Boulder, CO 80301 (303) 442-5828.

MARMOT MOUNTAIN WORKS, 3098 Marmot Lane, Grand Junction, CO 81504 (303) 434-6688.

MOTHER'S MOUNTAIN SUPPLY, Box 806, Gaithersburg, MD, 20877 (800) 638-4078.

THE NORTH FACE, 999 Harrison Street, Berkeley, CA 94710 (415) 527-9700.

OUTDOOR RESEARCH, 1000 1st Avenue South, Seattle, WA 98134 (206) 467-8197.

OUTFITTERS EXPRESS, 719 West Ellsworth, Ann Arbor, MI 48104 (800) 521-0549; in Michigan: (313) 769-5448.

PATAGONIA, Inc, PO Box 86, Ventura, CA 93002 (805) 648-3386.

REI (Recreational Equipment, Inc), PO Box C-88125, Seattle, WA 98188-0125 (800) 426-4840; in WA State: (800) 562-4894; in CA and Alaska: (206) 575-3287.

ROYAL ROBBINS, 1314 Coldwell Avenue, Modesto, CA 95350 (209) 529-6913.

SIERRA DESIGNS, 247 4th Street, Oakland, CA 94607 (415) 835-4950.

WILDERNESS EXPERIENCE, 20675 Nordhoff Street, Chatsworth, CA 91311 (800) 222-5725; in CA: (213) 998-3000.

Boot Repair
WHEELER & WILSON BOOTS, 206 North Main Street, Bishop, CA 93514 (619) 873-7520. Specialises in repair of all types of footwear, including hiking and skiing boots and climbing shoes.

Health Information Sources
US Public Health Service. Offers current information concerning disease prevalence worldwide. Available

by phone. Look in your local phone directory under US Government for the regional USPHS office. Or, contact the USPHS Foreign Quarantine Division at the nearest International Airport.

The USPHS booklet:

Health Information for International Travellers (stock no. 017-023-00173-6) gives recent data on required immunisations. This can be ordered for $3.25, prepaid, from the Superintendent of Documents, US Government Printing Office, Washington DC 20402 (202) 783-3238.

International Health Care Service, 440 East 69th Street, New York, New York 10021 (212) 472-4284. Offers individualised health counseling by tropical medicine specialists to people with specific itineraries. Normally conducted in person, exceptions can be made for counseling over the phone. The fee is $45.00 for counseling, additional charges are made if prescriptions and immunisations are given. Book available: *International Health Care: Travellers Guide* for $4.50 and a self-addressed, stamped envelope. Bulk rates are available for group orders.

International Association for Medical Assistance to Travellers (IAMAT), 735 Center Street, Lewiston, NY 14092 (716) 754-4883 or 188 Nicklin Road, Guelph, Ontario, Canada N1H 7L5 (519) 836-0102. A non-profit organisation/international network of health care centers and physicians in 125 countries and territories. Their directory of clinics is available by request as well as literature about health dangers abroad. No membership fee is required but donations are accepted.

First Aid Kits: Various types of ready-made first aid/ survival kits are available from the following companies among others. For a complete medical kit, you should discuss your needs with your personal physician and consult the medical books in the bibliographical section.

ADVENTURE 16, Outdoor Research, Outfitters Express, Brigade Quartermasters and REI. See addresses above.

Appendix 4: Expedition Food Suppliers

ALPINEAIRE FOODS, PO Box 926, Nevada City, CA 95959 (916) 272-1971. Mail order or call for nearby dealers.

BRIGADE QUARTERMASTERS, LTD, 266 Roswell Street, Marietta, GA 30060 (404) 428-1234.

DRI-LITE FOODS, Inc, 1540 Charles Drive, Redding, CA 96003 (800) 641-0500; in CA: (916) 241-9280.

OREGON FREEZE DRIED FOODS, Manufacturers of Mountain House Brand. PO Box 1048, Albany, OR 97321 (800) 547-4060. No mail order, but write or call for dealers near you.

RICH MOOR, 6923 Woodley Avenue, Van Nuys, CA 91406 (818) 787-2510.

WEE-PACK, Inc, 155 North Edison Way, Reno, NV 89502 (702) 786-4825. Sold through mail order or their retail outlet at the same address.

Appendix 5: A Rough Guide to Weights and Measures

(Reproduced with permission from the Expedition Advisory Centre's annual *Expedition Planner's Handbook and Directory*)

A 35 mm film container (they are watertight) holds:

2 ample servings of jam
3 ample servings of peanut butter
6 ample servings of sugar
4 ample servings of butter
2 large measures of whisky!

Some useful equivalents:

½ oz (15 g) sugar	1 level tablespoon
2 oz (55 g) syrup	1 tablespoon
6 oz (170 g) currants or raisins	1 level ½ pint (300 ml) mug
1 oz (30 g) flour	1 heaped tablespoon
½ oz (15 g) breadcrumbs	1 heaped tablespoon
½ pint (275 ml) dried milk	15 tablespoons
½ lb (225 g) sugar	1 level ½ pint (300 ml) mug
1 oz (30 g) fat	piece the size of large walnut
dehydrated egg	1 level tablespoon with 2 tablespoons of water=1 egg

A 1-pint (570 ml) ladle holds:

¾ lb (340 g) flour
6 oz (170 g) tea
1¼ lb (560 g) rice or pulses
1 lb (450 g) small dried fruit
1 lb 3 oz (535 g) sugar

The smaller half of a military-style mess tin holds approximately:

2 pints (generous 1 litre) liquid
1 lb 5 oz (590 g) flour
2½ lb (1,125 g) rice
1 lb 9 oz (735 g) oats
2 lb 6 oz (1,070 g) sugar

A standard dessertspoon when heaped holds about ½ oz (15 g) of light commodities and when level about ½ oz (15 g) of heavy commodities.

An average hen's egg weighs 2 oz (55 g).

A levelled serving spoon holds approximately:

1¼ oz (38 g) flour	1¾ oz (53 g) pulse
¾ oz (23 g) tea	1½ oz (45 g) rice
1½ oz (45 g) sugar	1 oz (30 g) oats

4 level serving spoons of liquid is equal to ¼ pint (150 ml).

A sardine/fish tin holds approximately:

3 oz (85 g) flour	6 oz (170 g) pulse
5½ oz (155 g) rice	5½ oz (155 g) sugar
3½ oz (100 g) oats	1¾ oz (53 g) tea

A normal can of tinned milk, or tin of equivalent size holds approximately:

8½ oz (240 g) flour	14 oz (400 g) pulse
14 oz (400 g) rice	14½ oz (415 g) sugar
9 oz (255 g) oats	4¾ oz (137 g) tea

Appendix 6: Some Useful Publications

Travel Advice

American Youth Hostel Association, National Administrative Offices, 1332 1 Street NW, Suite 800, Washington DC 20005 (202) 783-6161. Publishes the American Youth Hostel Handbook annually which includes a list of the 265 hostels in the US and all pertinent information. They also distribute a similar handbook for Canadian hostels as well as the International Youth Hostel Federation handbook mentioned in the bibliography. There is a small charge for these books unless you are a member of the association. Other brochures and books are also available. Many types of memberships are offered, ranging in price from $10 (for people under 17) to $200 for a life membership.

BRADT ENTERPRISES, Inc, 95 Harvy Street, Cambridge, MA 02140 (617) 492-8776. Produces excellent guides to South America including backpackers' guides and river travel advice. Sells maps and a number of books listed below.

SIERRA CLUB, 730 Polk Street, San Francisco, CA 94109 (415) 776-2211. Members receive, among other publications, an annual 'Outings' issue which can be quite informative.

Travel Publishers

ADVENTURE GUIDES, Inc, 36 East 57th Street, New York, New York 10022 (212) 355-6334.

BRADT ENTERPRISES, Inc, 95 Harvy Street, Cambridge, MA 02140 (617) 492-8776.

DAVID McKAY, 2 Park Avenue, New York, New York 10016 (212) 340-9800.

FODOR'S TRAVEL GUIDES, 2 Park Avenue, New York, New York 10016 (212) 340-9800.

LONELY PLANET, Box 2001A, Berkeley, CA 94702 (415) 525-5528.

MICHAEL CHESSLER MOUNTAINEERING BOOKS, 90 Hudson St, New York, New York 10013 (212) 219-1696. Not a publisher, but a mail-order house for travel and mountaineering books and publications. Particularly good for finding rare and out-of-print books.

THE MOUNTAINEERS, 306 2nd Avenue W., Seattle, WA 98119 (206) 285-2665.

RAND McNALLY, Box 7600, Chicago, IL 60680 (312) 673-9100, (800) 323-4070.

SIERRA CLUB BOOKS, 730 Polk Street, San Francisco, CA 94109 (415) 776-2211.

WILDERNESS PRESS, 2440 Bancroft Way, Berkeley, CA 94704 (415) 843-8080.

Travel and Outdoor Publications
Backpacker Magazine, 1515 Broadway, New York, New York 10036.
Outside Magazine, 1165 North Clark Street, Chicago, IL 60610.
Travel & Leisure, 1350 Avenue of the Americas, New York, New York 10019.
Diversion, 60 East 42nd Street, New York, New York 10165.
National Geographic Traveler, 17th and M Streets NW, Washington DC 20036.

Bibliography
Travel
Adventure Travel, by Pat Dickerman, Adventure Guides, Inc
The Adventurer's Guide, by Jack Wheeler, David McKay Company

The Adventurous Traveller's Guide, by Leo Le Bon, Simon & Schuster

China—Off the Beaten Track, by Brian Schwartz, St Martin's Press

The Complete Traveller, by Joan Bakewell, Beekman Publications

Expeditions: The Expert's Way, by John Blashford-Snell and Alastair Ballantine, Faber & Faber, in paperback

Francis Galton's Art of Travel, by Francis Galton, David & Charles

Guide to El Dorado and the Inca Empire, by Lynn Meisch, Penguin, in paperback

A Guide to Trekking in Nepal, by Stephen Bezruchka, The Mountaineers

Indonesian Handbook, by Bill Dalton, edited by Deke, Castleman, Moon Publications

India, a Practical Guide, by John Leak, Bradt Enterprises

International Youth Hostel Handbook: Africa, America, Asia, Australia. Published annually, available through the American Youth Hostel Association

Sahara Handbook, by Simon and Jan Glen, Bradt Enterprises

South American Explorer, by Bradt Enterprises

South American Survival, by Maurice Taylor, State Mutual Book

Travellers' Survival Kit to the East: Turkey, Iraq, Iran, Afghanistan, India, Nepal, Sri Lanka, Burma, by Susan Griffith, Bradt Enterprises

A Trekker's Guide to the Himalaya and Karakoram, by Hugh Swift, Sierra Club Books

The Tropical Traveller, by John Hatt, Hippocrene Books

The World Guide to Mountains and Mountaineering, by John Cleare, Smith Publications

Survival

Medicine for Mountaineering, edited by Dr James A. Wilkerson, The Mountaineers

Mountain Sickness—Prevention, Recognition and Treatment, by Dr Peter Hackett, The American Alpine Club

Mountaineering—The Freedom of the Hills, edited by
    P. Ferber, The Mountaineers
Stay Alive in the Desert, by Dr K. E. Melville, Bradt
    Enterprises
Staying Healthy in Asia, edited by Anne Huckins.
    Stanford: Volunteers in Asia. Order from: VIA, Box
    4543, Stanford, CA 94305. Include a check for $2.50
    plus tax, plus $1.50 for postage
The Traveller's Health Guide, by Dr A. C. Turner, Bradt
    Enterprises

Bush Cookery
Backpacker's Cookbook, by Margaret Cross and Jean
    Fiske, Ten-Speed Press, in paperback
*The Complete Light-pack Camping and Trail Foods
    Cookbook*, by E. P. Drew, McGraw-Hill Paperbacks
Gorp, Glop and Glue Stew, by Yvonne Prater and Ruth
    Dyar, Mendenhall, The Mountaineers
Simple Foods for the Pack, by Vicki Kinmont and Claudia
    Axcell, Sierra Club Books